Praise f

"Wired for God is vibrating with light. Dani is a wonderful, compassionate healer and she shares her inspiring journey with so much love. This book is not to be missed."

—Diane Goldner, healer and author of *A Call to Heal: A Spiritual Memoir* and *Yes, You Can Heal*

"Dani Antman invites us along on her wondrous journey of spiritual awakening. Her story is an inner journey of self-discovery, profound healing, fierce honesty and startling transformation. Along the way we are given glimpses into the profound mysteries of that Unity which holds us all. This is a book that will inspire us to persevere through every resistance, and let the deepest wisdom of our hearts guide us Home."

—Rabbi Shefa Gold, Director of The Center for Devotional, Energy and Ecstatic Practice

"If you are drawn to the big questions in life, if you are beginning or continuing your own spiritual journey, please read *Wired for God*. Through her insights into Kabbalah and Kundalini, the author comes close to naming the un-nameable, expertly weaving mystical experiences into daily life."

—Donna Baier Stein, founder of the Tiferet Journal and author of *The Silver Baron's Wife*

"[*Wired for God is*] a remarkably colorful, candid, and truly insightful, inspirational account of Dani's life, loves, learnings and breakthroughs. The revelations by Dani and her teachers help us celebrate the wondrous power of This One Divine Power doing everything and being everyone *Jai Jagadambe Ma* and *Baruch Ha-Shem*!

—Timothy Conway, PhD, author of *Women of Power and Grace: Nine Astonishing, Inspiring Luminaries of Our Time*

"Everyone is wired for God, but wiring alone isn't enough. You have to throw the switch and turn on the power. Dani Antman has done both. *Wired for God* is a wonderful testament to Dani's spiritual journey. Just don't forget to walk the path yourself."

—Rabbi Rami Shapiro, author of The World Wisdom Bible

Wired for God

Adventures of a Jewish Yogi

DANI ANTMAN

TURNING
STONE
PRESS

Cover design by Frame25 Productions
Cover art by Katyau, c/o Shutterstock.com
Interior design by Howie Severson
Interior Mandala Design by Cynthia Lee
Author Photo by Madeleine Vite

Turning Stone Press
8301 Broadway St., Ste. 219
San Antonio, TX 78209

Library of Congress Control Number
is available upon request.

ISBN: 978-1-61852-116-3

10 9 8 7 6 5 4 3 2 1

Printed in the United States of America

*This book is my deep bow of gratitude
to all the teachers who have guided me
on the spiritual path and to the lineages
behind them.*

*In memory of Swamiji Chandrasekharanand
Saraswati. Your dedication, integrity,
and intense love for the Divine have
inspired me. Your knowledge of Kundalini
Shakti has liberated me from the bondage
of the past. Your deep desire to share
the practical application of your knowledge
has changed my life forever.*

Contents

Foreword

by Marci Shimoff

When I first met Dani Antman, I instantly recognized a fellow spiritual seeker, someone fiercely devoted to self-realization and the spiritual path. We were both studying with a realized Swami, the founder of Patanjali Kundalini Yoga Care (PKYC). Dani and I bonded over our Jewish backgrounds, our mutual interest in Kabbalah, our similar challenges on the spiritual path, and our commitment to finding true methods for experiencing Oneness consciousness.

The spiritual guidance I received at PKYC and the improvement of my Kundalini process helped me move beyond the conditioning that had blocked my happiness. This transformation was huge for me and ultimately led me to write my best-selling books *Happy for No Reason* and *Love for No Reason*.

Dani also experienced a personal awakening that she shares in these pages. Her engaging and candid story speaks to the challenges we all face when we want to connect with the Divine, and to the power of self-forgiveness and faith on our journey. This moving memoir clearly shows that we are all wired for God.

There are very few accounts of spiritual awakening written by women, and, to my knowledge, this is the first to explore the unique combination of Jewish mysticism and Kundalini Science. Dani reconciles these two seemingly disparate approaches by showing how the inner force that drives our human evolution—whether you call it *Shakti,* the Holy Spirit, or *Shekinah*—is truly "God within." When tapped into through practice, this force can bring a person into direct union with the Divine.

In our modern world, where rituals of initiation have been mostly eliminated, and where religious leaders aren't necessarily initiated themselves, we've lost many of the traditional guideposts to spiritual development. Dani's story of spiritual opening is authentic; her wisdom about how to discern true spiritual progress is both valuable and enlightening.

It's inspiring to recognize that the path to self-realization is built right into our DNA, just waiting to be activated. If you follow your sincere desire to know God, you can trust your inner guidance to take you home to the Divine. There are no wrong turns, only important lessons. And, as Dani found, home is a far more magical place than you could have imagined.

Wired for God is for anyone on the path of consciousness. Whether you're a beginner or a seasoned practitioner, this story will shine light on what is so often overlooked: you can't make a wrong turn when you're truly seeking God.

May you be inspired to continue on your path, no matter how winding—and may you come home to your Divine light within.

Namaste, Shalom, and Blessings,
Marci

Marci Shimoff is the #1 *New York Times* best-selling author of *Happy for No Reason, Love for No Reason,* and *Chicken Soup for the Woman's Soul.*

Introduction

What are the odds of an ordinary Jewish girl from Queens, New York, meeting a realized Indian Master from Rishi-kesh, India, steeped in the esoteric knowledge of yoga, Vedanta, Kundalini Science, and, most surprisingly, the Jewish mystical path of Kabbalah. Well, I would say pretty slim!

Wired for God: Adventures of a Jewish Yogi is a memoir of my search for personal healing and spiritual awakening. My spiritual path emerged from the confluence of three esoteric traditions: Yogic Science, Kundalini Science, and Kabbalah. Paradoxically, this combination led me to a triumphant return to the religion of my birth, Judaism.

Religions provide the *preliminary* practices to walk a spiritual path through guidelines for right behavior, ethics, and morality. However, in today's world, they don't provide the individual guidance and practices needed to help advanced spiritual seekers stabilize in Unitive consciousness.

I am telling my story to inspire spiritual seekers of all traditions to persevere on the spiritual path, which can often get discouraging without the right guidance. My story demonstrates that as you open spiritually, your path is guided from within by grace, and the right teacher will appear. I candidly share my own inner experiences as I transform from a New York City party girl to energy healer and then to dedicated spiritual seeker. I also recount my struggles with the pitfalls commonly encountered by all spiritual seekers, such as ego inflation, seduction, disillusionment, and pride. My hope is that my story will help you steer clear of these obstacles or face them head on in your own life.

Have you ever wondered what happens inside you to create sustained spiritual awareness? Or wonder if the spiritual practices to which you are devoted are actually effective? And if so, how do they work? In my effort to find the answers to these questions, I read every account of spiritual awakening that I could find, searching for guidance and direction. I wondered why some people awaken suddenly, while others meditate for many years and still feel stuck.

Nondual spiritual teachers in the West promote the idea that we just have to *awaken to who we already are* and that spiritual practices are not necessary. While this may be true for the rare few, it has not been my experience. My spiritual journey demonstrates a path of gradual spiritual progress, facilitated by right support, persistence, and the correct practices. In this way, I was slowly prepared for sustained contact with the Divine.

You and I are wired for this profound transformation of consciousness. The wiring is in your subtle body, the network of energy channels that surrounds and interpenetrates your physical body. The subtle body is the blueprint for your life. It is powered from within by the Divine feminine force of awakening, called Kundalini Shakti in yoga or Shekinah in Kabbalah. No matter what her name, she is the inner power within every spiritual path that, when aroused, works relentlessly to transform you from the inside out to become a fit vessel for God consciousness. I experienced this profound process of awakening and hope that my story illuminates specific aspects of your own journey, enabling you to have more discernment and clarity on your spiritual path.

My story unfolds in three parts:

In part 1, Discovery and Doubt, I relate my earliest spiritual stirrings from childhood to young adulthood, as I encounter the wounds of my Jewish heritage—mixed with confusion and shame. As an adult, I become fascinated by esoteric phenomena such as channeling, past lives, and clairvoyance, and I take an inspired leap of faith and become an energy healer. I quickly find out that the first step on the healing path is: *Healer, heal thyself.* So I commence the ultimate journey, the journey inward toward self-knowledge. While opening to the subtle realms of energy and light, I struggle with my human imperfections, my projections, and my shadow. A healing crisis, seduction by a dark teacher, and the dissolution of my marriage propel me to search for a spiritual path.

In part 2, Kabbalah: The Jewish Mystical Path, I am introduced to the study of the often cryptic and hard-to-understand teachings of Kabbalah. I learn an exciting new paradigm of healing rooted in a nondualistic view of the Tree of Life that radically shifts my understanding of healing. I perceive the wholeness that includes all opposites, and I discover more capacity to be with all of life just as it is. The Kabbalistic teachings come alive under my hands as I learn to use the *sefirot*, the ten Divine attributes of the Tree of Life, for healing. I face a spiritual crisis when I struggle to do advanced practices created by my teacher, and I have to choose between my inner guidance and outer success. I pray for help and a new path appears.

In part 3, Kundalini: The Vedic Path to Enlightenment, I miraculously meet Swamiji, an Indian Master in a lineage of Kundalini Science, who offers me the precise guidance I need to advance spiritually. I discover that my own style of Kundalini rising is the difficult Vajra rising, common to Jewish seekers. This rising brings great esoteric gifts but will not culminate in self-realization. A Vajra rising does, however, explain my sexual propensities, exhaustion, and lack of spiritual progress.

On my first retreat, I experience a correction of the Vajra process and the sacred arrival at *Makara* point, the real beginning of spiritual life. I finally learn practices that renovate and restore my previously damaged subtle body and lead to the permanent improvement of my spiritual process. For more than fourteen years, I dig deeply in one place and eventually have a culminating experience of Unitive consciousness. The irony of my loyalty to this one path and teacher is that it brings me full circle back to Judaism and the path of Kabbalah, now enriched and expanded by knowledge and experience.

If there is one message I want to deliver in this book, it is this: If you are on a spiritual path, don't give up until you reap the rewards of your practice. Every sincere seeker, longing for liberation, is helped by the Divine within and by the adepts who oversee all the great spiritual traditions, who witness your holy yearning and answer your call. Just remember the old adage: you may have to knock three times before the door is opened. May your journey of transformation unfold gracefully through your own soul's guidance.

Prologue

Queens, New York, 1961

The limo pulled up to the steps of the big Catholic church near Corporal Kennedy Street. The church dwarfed the small, redbrick, two-family houses that populated the quiet Queens neighborhood where I lived. Every Saturday, I gathered with a few older kids to await the arrival of the weekend's bride.

Watching her emerge from her limo like an exotic princess was our form of wondrous entertainment. She floated up the church steps, flanked by her ladies-in-waiting, diaphanous white gown trailing behind her, face hidden behind a veil. She looked oh so old and sophisticated to my five-year-old eyes. Like every little girl, I imagined my own wedding day, playing out this scene with my Barbie doll thousands of times, never getting tired of the grand event.

On one such Saturday, we watched the procession, following the bride as she disappeared through the immense church doors that closed behind her. Curious to find out what would happen next, together we pulled on the iron handles to crack open the massive wooden church doors for a peek.

Inside the dark, cavernous interior of the church, the drone of murmured chanting and the smell of incense created an exotic and foreign atmosphere. I stood on my tippy toes to look for the bride, but she was nowhere to be seen. My eyes drifted upward toward the carving of a tortured, dying man nailed to a wooden cross, high up on the far wall, hovering over the congregation. I wondered who he was and why he looked so twisted and in such pain.

I couldn't take my eyes off him. My chest tightened, and in that moment the bubble of my innocence was shattered. I felt an overwhelming sadness, too heavy for my five years of age. For the first time in my young life, a feeling of compassion arose in my heart, as if I could see into this man's heart and feel his pain. Suddenly, a dark-robed figure strode over and shooed us outside as he pulled the heavy doors shut.

I realize now that this incident remains in my memory as my first spiritual experience. It connected me to something larger than myself through my heart. The big themes of life, death, suffering, and the mysterious union of the masculine and feminine are embedded in this memory.

Back outside in the sunlight, we waited for what seemed like hours to shower the bride and groom with rice when they emerged. I turned to my friend Jessica and asked, "Who is the man on the cross?"

She replied, "That's Jesus. He is the son of God, and the Jews killed him."

I was bewildered by her answer. I knew I was Jewish, but why would my people kill this man? I didn't want to be "Jewish" if it had anything to do with the pain of the man on the cross. For some inexplicable reason, I felt ashamed. Later, I told my mom what had happened.

"We are Jewish," she replied curtly. "We don't go to church, and we don't worship Jesus. We go to synagogue.

And I don't want you hanging out at that church anymore!"

How could God have a son, and why would someone want to kill him? What did that have to do with being Jewish? Later someone told me that Jesus himself was Jewish, and I became even more confused. Only many years after did I understand the real story of Jesus.

I ignored my mother and went back to the church again and again, as my fascination with the bride became secondary to my need to see inside the church and understand its mystery. That first glimpse of Jesus on the cross planted a seed in my heart to discover the inner meaning of religion and spirituality, although I didn't know it then.

When something is named, it becomes distinct, it can be described, it has qualities. Religion is like that, channeling the unnameable presence into a form that could be touched, named, and qualified. At its best, religion creates rituals to help us experience the ineffable. At its worst, it causes separation, war, and hatred. It is not a surprise that after this early experience, I grew up with an ambivalent relationship toward my Jewish religion.

Part I

Discovery and Doubt

I

Growing Up Jewish

Queens, New York, 1960s

There is a crack in everything, that's how the light gets in.
—Leonard Cohen

I was raised culturally Jewish but not religious.

My dad, a child of Polish immigrants, came from an observant family. He grew up in a Brooklyn ghetto, and his mom kept a kosher kitchen. His parents spoke Yiddish, and consequently my childhood was peppered with Yiddish words used when my parents didn't want us kids, myself and my younger brother and sister, to understand what they were saying.

Words that remain in my vocabulary and still tickle my ears when I say them are:

- *meshugunna*—crazy

- *bubbemyseh*—an old wives' tale

- *tsurris*—big trouble

- *fermisht*—all shook up

- *ferdrayt*—dizzy and confused

- *oy gevalt*—how terrible

Strung together into a sentence, they might sound something like this: "That *meshugunna* lady down the block, she tells such *bubbemysehs* to all you kids. Don't listen to her! It will only make *tsurris!* You will become *fermisht* and *ferdrayt, oy gevalt!*"

When my dad joined the navy at age seventeen, he was the only Jew on his ship, and he abandoned his religious observances so as not to be ostracized.

My mom was brought up in the Bronx by parents who felt being "American" was more important than being Jewish. My mom's father owned a small store and was a pharmacist, so they had some financial security. Both of my parents grew up during the Great Depression, and the insecurity of those times imprinted upon them the desire to create a safe and secure life for their children.

In our home, Jewish holiday celebrations centered on food: *matzo* ball soup at Passover, potato *latkes* at Channukah, and *hamentashen*, a prune or poppy pastry in the shape of a triangle, at Purim. We hardly ever observed the rituals of the religion and attended synagogue only once or twice a year.

I did, however, learn the Jewish prohibitions: Do not date Gentile boys, do not eat shellfish or ham, do not shop on Saturdays, and do not have Christmas or believe in Jesus. Somehow the rules were bent for shopping and eating shellfish, but not for dating Gentile boys, believing in Jesus, nor celebrating Christmas.

Wired for God

Becoming Aware of the World

In the 1960s, an atmosphere of fear from the Holocaust still permeated the Jewish culture. Although I learned about the Holocaust in grade school, I didn't fully comprehend the impact of what had happened until much later, at my first real job when I was nineteen. I was hired by the Lucius N. Littauer Foundation, a foundation that supported Jewish education, to catalogue mountains of old clippings and pamphlets that the president, Harry Starr, had collected for more than forty years. One day, I came across newspaper clippings from the years 1938 to 1945. I hardly got any work done as I instead read the *New York Times* articles chronicling Hitler's growing threat and his attempts to annihilate the Jewish people. My horror grew as I read the articles, living through the news as if those events were unfolding in current time. In hindsight, it is no accident that I developed debilitating migraines that year and eventually quit the job.

But as a young child growing up in the '60s, those events were not part of my consciousness. When the Six-Day War started in Israel in 1967, all the neighbors rallied to collect money to support the Jewish state. The battle for the State of Israel seemed distant compared to the Vietnam War, which was played out in our living room every night on the evening news. I tuned out the images of violence and couldn't imagine the young boys on my block being drafted and sent off to the jungles of Vietnam. My first day of junior high school, students held a "sit-in" to protest the war.

By the time I was twelve, drugs had infiltrated the neighborhood, and my "older friends"—who were all of fourteen—were already smoking pot and using LSD. To add to the atmosphere of instability, the serial killer Son of Sam was on the loose, and several of his murders happened nearby. Despite these chaotic times, my parents did their best to create a stable home and imprint upon us the desire for a college education, a successful career, and marriage to a Jewish partner, preferably a doctor or a lawyer for me.

Religious education was optional for me, mandatory for my brother. When asked if I wanted to go to Hebrew school so that I could have a bat mitzvah, the coming of age ceremony given for thirteen-year-old girls in the Jewish tradition, I declined. I shrank inwardly at the thought of standing in front of my friends and family and reading from the Torah in Hebrew. I also knew that my parents couldn't afford more than one extravagant party, and my brother's bar mitzvah was the priority.

Nevertheless, I remember my excitement when I was invited to my first big bar mitzvah party by of one of the most popular boys in my class. My mom fussed with my hair as she pinned large curls on top of my head and weaved them into a multilevel beehive. I wore a pretty brown and pink chiffon minidress, a hand-me-down because we didn't have the money for new clothes at the time. My excitement about the party was tinged with guilt, because I knew that giving a monetary gift to the boy would stretch my parent's limited budget.

A Crack in My World

Around the time I was just entering adolescence, my parents were engaged in an epic financial battle with my maternal grandparents. My grandparents wanted to retire and move to Florida. They were determined to extract every penny they could from my parents as they negotiated the sale of the attached two-family home that they co-owned and the business that they had groomed my father to run.

My grandfather's business had changed from owning a pharmacy to manufacturing creams, lotions, and perfumes for distribution to smaller companies. He had taught my dad, who, though not a pharmacist, learned how to mix the ingredients from the formulas and then create, fill, and package the products. My dad always came home smelling like his latest creation, and I came to love perfume, associating it with the smell of my father.

Our house shared an interior door with my grandparents, who lived upstairs. The door was always open, and, as a child, every night I scrambled upstairs after dinner to join them for a second supper. My favorite meal was *matzo brie*, a kind of Jewish French toast. I stood on a stool and watched my grandmother first soak the matzo cracker in water, then squeeze it dry and plunge it into beaten egg. The combination was then scrambled until it became fluffy and lightly browned. I waited impatiently for it to be ready, my mouth watering as I anticipated dipping the cooked morsels into sugar, sour cream, or applesauce.

Now it was my parents who headed up the stairs every night to my grandparents' quarters to negotiate the terms of the sale. I sat scrunched up on the steps with my ear pressed to the adjoining wall, trying to get a handle on why my mother and grandmother were screaming at each other. Picture a Jewish version of the TV show *Dynasty*, with Crystal and Alexis, well-matched adversaries, engaged in a life-or-death duel of words.

"You are cheating us!" my mother yelled in a raspy voice. "We could never pay that much money for the business. The house isn't worth what you want for it!

What do you want to do, ruin our lives? Don't you care about your grandchildren?"

My grandmother shouted back, "Do you want us to starve in Florida? We can't live on what you are offering us! We'll sell the business to someone else!"

Back and forth they went for hours, and then my parents came downstairs, drained of all color, and retreated to their bedroom.

The nightly, high-decibel screaming matches continued for months and were impossible to ignore. As the oldest child, I was the one who was supposed to be in charge, and I resented it. I fought constantly with my younger brother and sister, as if we could transmute the energy and tension in the house by staging our own battles.

My friends asked, "How come you don't speak to your grandparents anymore?" I felt ashamed and couldn't explain the situation, because I didn't really understand what was happening myself.

My friends and I stole Newport Light cigarettes from an unsuspecting mom, and we smoked endlessly. Inhaling the cool menthol smoke tickled my nose and became a balm to my feelings of despair.

I became obsessed with a boy across the street. Tall and lanky, he had a ponytail and a great sense of humor. Two years older than me (not Jewish, of course), he had a reputation as a "bad boy" because he rode minibikes, smoked, and did drugs.

The atmosphere in his house was worse than it was in mine. We crept past his alcoholic mother in his perennially dark house and spent hours kissing in his bedroom. Fevered embraces, tongues exploring, we found every possible way to rub each other, without taking off our clothes. Overwhelmed with lust, I lived in a constant fantasy world anticipating our next meeting.

My dad lost twenty pounds and paced around the house muttering to himself. During the day, he went to work with my grandfather as if everything were okay. At night, the fights resumed, and it was like living in a war zone.

Speaking to my grandparents soon started to feel like a betrayal of my parents. Gradually, we three kids ignored them, even though we shared the same driveway and would see them coming and going. I no longer ran up the stairs excited to share my day with them. Pulled between two sides like a child of divorce, how could I choose my grandparents over my parents? My grandparents became the enemy.

This was the setting for my adolescence, and my excitement about going to a bar mitzvah was overshadowed by guilt because things were so tense at home. My dad looked at me all dressed up, a budding young lady, and, with his voice choking, said, "You will always be my little girl. Come, I will drive you to the synagogue."

As we pulled up, he parked the car, and with tears in his eyes he turned to me. "We finally settled with your grandparents. They will move to Florida, and we will own the business and the house. I don't know how we're going to make it. I owe the bank two hundred thousand dollars for the settlement. You kids may not have what you want, but you will have what you need. I'll make sure of that. We're going to be okay. We're a family, and we will get through this together," he reassured me. Far from being reassured, I felt shaken and scared. I had never seen my father cry before.

My heart broke as I hugged him goodbye and went into the synagogue in a daze. I sat down in the row with all my friends. They were exchanging glances, admiring and comparing their party dresses. I felt as if I were falling into an abyss, wondering how my family was ever going to survive.

The service started, and when the words of the *Shema* were chanted, everything seemed to disappear. Tears rolled down my face as the ancient chant of unity permeated my being. My worries and fears were subsumed in the chanting: *Shema Y'Israel Adonai Eloheynu Adonai Echad.* Listen Israel, you who wrestle with God, God is One.

I didn't know the Hebrew prayer or what the words meant then, but I experienced them as balm to my aching soul. They spoke to a union beyond the world of battling matriarchs and irreconcilable opposites; they soothed me, and, for a brief moment, I felt something ineffable, as if I were in the presence of God.

Many years later I received an envelope from my grandmother. Inside were pictures of all of us during better times. There was a short note: *Don't you remember us? We love you. Call us.*

But I couldn't do it. I couldn't contact them and forge my own adult relationship with them without feeling I was betraying my parents. My parents never saw them again, despite the fact that they, too, eventually moved to Florida. My grandparents both died without ever reconciling with our family.

This painful episode caused a crack in my world that I didn't know how to repair and left me with a strong belief that conflicts can be resolved only through painful separation. It is probably this early rupture in my family that eventually led me in my adult years to explore the healing arts and energy work.

2

From Artist to Healer

New York City, 1986–1988

*The first thing you will face after committing yourself to
your path is your fear.*

—Barbara Ann Brennan

New York City was *the* place to be in the 1980s. After graduating from the New York School of Interior Design, I rented
my own miniscule apartment on the Upper West Side, living the life of a single, New York City party girl, very much
like Carrie Bradshaw, the character Sarah Jessica Parker
played in *Sex in the City*. I spent summer weekends on Fire
Island or in the Hamptons; I had a long list of sizzling and
short relationships; I smoked, drank, and danced all night
in the afterhours clubs. I took multiple trips to Europe
where I did the very same activities. The only thing I didn't
have was Carrie's budget for clothes and shoes.

I barely attended Jewish services or thought about
Judaism, other than the ever-present command to marry
a Jewish man. I rebelled and dated men from every other
possible religion and nationality to be found in the
bars and clubs of New York City. Looking back, I led a

promiscuous and superficial life. It is no excuse that all my friends were doing the same thing, or that it was a sign of the times: the post-60s, feminist, sexual liberation, pre-AIDS, Studio 54 days.

My spiritual self bubbled under the surface, and I satisfied my curiosity by being an armchair traveler: I read books. I gravitated toward books about magical powers and esoteric spiritual paths. Once, when I was nine or ten, my dad had brought home some books that he happened to be shipping for a mail-order company. The books were on telekinesis, the ability to move objects with one's will, and astral traveling, the ability to leave one's body consciously. With great excitement, I carefully studied the books and tried all the exercises they presented in an attempt to move an object with my mind or to leave my body. I just ended up with a big headache and gave up.

Later, I became obsessed with Carlos Castaneda's series of books that describe his esoteric training under the tutelage of the shaman Don Juan Matus. I desperately wanted to experience the alternate realities he described, most of which were induced by plant medicine or by direct transmission from his teacher. I had a secret desire to meet someone just like Don Juan, who would train me to perceive subtle levels of reality. I never consciously thought that I would undertake such training.

By the time I graduated from interior design school, I knew I did not want to be an interior designer. Since I could read blueprints, I was employed and trained by the largest painting company in New York City to estimate the cost of their large commercial paint and wall-covering jobs. Although estimating jobs was not my passion, it gave me the time to go back to night school to study interior rendering, which is the art of creating perspective paintings to depict and sell the yet-to-be-built layouts of interior designers.

I loved that work and, within two years, I launched my own freelance art business, with barely five hundred dollars in the bank and a small portfolio from the class. I gradually built my business up, and after five years of struggling, I had a steady stream of clients who were the top interior designers in the field. I finally felt stable in my life, and I could pay attention to the voice inside me that whispered, "It's time to settle down and get married."

It seemed to be the next logical step.

Magically, I met Reuben soon after I made the inner decision to stop going for the "bad boys" and to find a man who would make a good husband.

One day, I glanced up from the painting in progress on my drafting table to see a tall, handsome man in a European-style navy overcoat peering into the window of my storefront office. I cracked the door open to see what he wanted.

"I am an architect, and I heard you have office space for rent here. Can I come in and look around?" he asked.

I blurted out, "You look so familiar. Have we met before?"

"No," he replied. (Later, he told me he had followed me once at the flea market.)

He had a kind, open face and didn't seem dangerous, so I let him in. The landlord wasn't around, so I showed him the various cubicles available for rent.

We both felt an immediate connection, as if we already knew each other. He told me about graduating at the top of his class as an architect from Cooper Union. I told him about my training in interior design. It turned out that I knew his last girlfriend, who had graduated from the New York School of Interior Design the year before me.

Although he didn't take the office space, he left saying, "Let's have lunch sometime; we have a lot in common." We started dating immediately.

Reuben was intelligent, grounded, smart, sweet, genuinely kind, family oriented—and Jewish! He had a strong physical resemblance to the poet Rimbaud and a similar sensitive nature. I chose him because he was exactly the opposite of the noncommittal playboys I had been dating.

He had grown up in New York City and had a very tight-knit relationship with his parents and brother, who all lived within blocks of one another on the Upper West Side. As I got to know him, I experienced the warmth of his family's relationship to Judaism, through the Shabbat dinners and Jewish holidays I celebrated with them. They were not overly religious but kept the holidays with an appreciation that can come only if you have been persecuted for your religion. Both of Reuben's parents were Holocaust survivors.

His Hungarian mom and Czechoslovakian dad had met in their late teens, while running from the Nazis. They fell in love as they fled their homes and their countries together, finally landing in Paris. They were first cousins, and they lost their entire family in the Holocaust, with the exception of one sibling each. Being with them gave me a new appreciation of Judaism and started to open my heart to its observances.

After two years of dating, just after my thirtieth birthday, Reuben and I got engaged. Our parents finally met one another, and we started planning our wedding. I imagined myself walking down the aisle as the bride in the white dress, the fantasy scene from my childhood finally coming true. The wedding symbolized my true entry into adulthood, even though I was already in my thirties. I was about to get married, my career was going well, and everything in my life felt as if it were on track.

Encounter with a Channeler

One day, I strode down Broadway, and a flyer taped to the clear side panel of a bus stop caught my eye. I stopped to read it.

DIANA MUENZ, TRANCE CHANNELER: CHANNELED WISDOM FROM ARCHANGEL MICHAEL AND LADY DIANA, declared the headline.

By coincidence, I had just finished reading Shirley MacLaine's book, *Out on a Limb*, where she describes her sessions with channeler Kevin Ryerson, whose spirit guides channel information to her about her past lives, the nature of reality, and God. Shirley MacLaine's openness about her spiritual quest and her explorations in those realms gave me the courage to even consider calling Diana. I had never seen a psychic or an astrologer before, let alone someone who claimed to speak with unseen beings from the other side.

Impulsively, I tore the flyer off the bus stop and decided that I would call her for an appointment as soon as I got home. At the time, I was interested in hearing about my upcoming marriage and finding out if Reuben and I had shared any past lives together; I didn't feel that I needed any particular advice. I didn't want anything in my life to change; I simply felt intrigued by the concept of channeling and wondered what I would learn from these nonphysical entities.

I waited in nervous anticipation for the appointed time. When I told Reuben I was going to see a channeler, he looked at me as if I were a bit askew but didn't say much.

The appointed day arrived, and I took the subway down to Diana's small walk-up apartment in Greenwich Village. I climbed the stairs and knocked on her door. A small-boned, beautiful woman with dark hair and soft, luminous eyes opened the door. I followed her through a fabric-draped opening into her small office and sat down opposite her.

"Have you ever had a channeled reading before?" she asked.

"No," I answered.

She explained, "I channel two main guides who enter my body and speak in different voices. I allow my personality to step back, and they take over my voice and body. I often don't remember what is said in a session, and I will make a tape for you so that you can listen to the reading again at home. My main guide, Lady Diana"—not the princess, who wouldn't be a public figure till many years later—"is an aspect of my higher self, and she speaks with an English accent. She will answer any personal questions you have. I also channel universal wisdom from Archangel Michael."

With that short introduction, she proceeded to recite an invocation to clear the space and begin our session:

"Father, Mother, God, we ask just now that Light of the highest vibration fill, surround, and protect us on all levels and all planes in accordance with your will."

Her body became still and went flaccid for a few short moments. Then, like a puppet coming to life, she inhaled sharply and Lady Diana, or Lady D for short, took over her movements and voice.

Even with her lilting English accent, it seemed quite normal to talk to her, as if I were conversing over a cup of tea with a wise old auntie who could see through the veneer of my personality to my soul.

She must have said some things about my marriage and my career; however, the only thing that I remember from that reading is one simple sentence that changed my life: "I see you have very sensitive hands, and your purpose in this life is to be a healer."

"A healer!" I exclaimed. "What's that? I paint pictures; I am an artist. Is that what you mean by having sensitive hands?"

"No, you could be an energy healer. Someone who can feel and transmit energy through their hands to help others."

I was incredulous. "An energy healer! That's not how I see myself."

"Well, dear, why don't you go to a new age bookstore and find a book about hands-on healing. See if it resonates with you. Do you have any further questions?"

I was so stunned that I couldn't think of any.

Shortly after that, the normal Diana came back into her body and yawned. She gracefully concluded the session, and I left her apartment astonished and intrigued by the thought that I could be a healer.

Hands of Light

Over the next few days, I toyed with the idea of finding a book on energy healing, and I finally consulted the yellow pages, where I discovered a prominent ad for the Samuel Weiser Bookstore, purveyor of spiritual and esoteric books since 1926.

The Samuel Weiser Bookstore was an emporium for every type of esoteric and occult book ever printed. As I entered the doors, I looked with amazement at the stacked shelves radiating vibrations from texts both ancient and new on Egyptian symbolism, Celtic spirituality, magic, theosophy, Goddess worship, crystals, tarot, Paganism, and so on. I didn't have to look long for books on healing. Just knowing that so many books existed on these subjects legitimized my search.

I glanced around and saw a book prominently displayed on the front table. The cover illustration showed blue hands, emanating streams of white light. The author, Barbara Ann Brennan, formerly a research scientist in atmospheric physics who had worked at NASA, had just published *Hands of Light*, which was to become a seminal book on energy healing. I stared at it, picked it up, then put it down and walked away. As I walked around, no other book on healing drew my attention, so I wandered back, picked it up again, and started reading.

I glanced at the first chapter, where Barbara describes a session with her first client, whom she called Jenny:

> I scanned her energy field, or aura, using my High Sense Perception (HSP). I "saw" some abnormal cells inside the uterus on the lower left side. At the same time, I "saw" the circumstances around the miscarriage. The abnormal cells were located where the placenta had been attached. I also "heard" words that described Jenny's condition and what to do about it.

As I read her words, a flash of lightening zigzagged through my nervous system, as if confirming that I had found the right book.

Barbara talked about her ability to see inside a person's body with her X-ray vision as if it were the most normal thing in the world! I wondered about her use of the terms "energy field" and "High Sense Perception" and whether I could learn how to see inside the body and channel energy from my hands for healing. I bought the book and plunged into the text.

By the time I finished the first three chapters, I understood that everything in creation has an energy field and that the human energy field surrounds and penetrates our physical body. The human energy field is formed at conception and is influenced by our thoughts, emotions, and beliefs. Universal energy can be transmitted to the human energy field by a trained healer through the laying on of hands for the purpose of healing.

The awareness of this energy field, sometimes called the *subtle body* or *aura,* is not new; most of the spiritual paths refer to it using different terms: the *most sacred body* and *true and genuine body* in Sufism, the *diamond body* in Taoism, the *light body* or *rainbow body* in Tibetan Buddhism, the *Tree of Life* in the Jewish Mystical Path of the Kabbalah, the *subtle body* in yoga, and the *immortal body* in Hermeticism.

Barbara presented a methodical way of learning how to perceive energy fields and auras and how to influence them for the purpose of healing. She described a progressive training to cultivate awareness beyond three-dimensional reality and linear time. It seemed to be a modern-day version of what Don Juan had offered to Carlos Castaneda!

I loved Barbara's scientific approach and, recalling Lady Diana's words to me, I called her office to see if I could book an appointment for a healing. By some great stroke of luck her secretary answered and immediately switched me to Barbara's personal line.

"This is Barbara Brennan speaking."

I stammered out, "My name is Dani, and I've just read your book. Can I come see you for a healing?"

"Are you sick? Why do you want to come?"

"No," I responded, "I am not sick. I read your book, and I have to meet you. I am fascinated by your description of energy fields and healing." I felt self-conscious and wondered whether she was seeing into my body or energy field as we spoke.

"Well," she told me, "I am closing up my New York City healing practice and opening a school on Long Island in order to train healers. It starts in a few weeks. Why don't you join us for the introductory weekend?"

"I'll think about it," I said, as a rush of excitement flooded my body.

I had never done anything like this, but I immediately knew that I wanted to go. I started planning how to rearrange my schedule and find the money to attend.

When I got home, I told Reuben that I wanted to go away for the weekend to study with a healer, and again he glanced at me with disbelief, but to his credit he didn't stop me. In fact, he encouraged me to do what I felt called to do.

I called my parents and told them about my new adventure. They both got on the phone at once, bombarding me with questions.

"What is this, some sort of cult? Who is this lady? Is she some sort of psychic? How much is she charging for this?"

"That stuff is all bullshit," my father said. "What are you wasting your money for?"

"Dad, I don't think it's bullshit," I countered, "She really helps people. I think I may want to do what she does." I hung up the phone determined to go and made arrangements for hotel accommodations and transportation.

Fasten Your Seat Belt!

The introductory weekend took place at the Bridge Hampton Community House, a large, shingled building with white shutters on the main street of what was actually Sag Harbor, New York. I barely slept the night before class. I dressed and arrived early that first morning, surprised to see more than one hundred attendees already milling about on the lawn outside. From the states written on their name tags along with their names, I could tell that they hailed from all over the United States.

I recognized Barbara immediately as she supervised the chairs and tables being unloaded and carried inside by her assistants. She wore a red, sleeveless, silk shirt, and her long thin legs descended from white shorts. Though dressed casually, she was clearly the one in charge. Her shoulder-length blond hair looked like it had been softly curled that morning and contrasted with her piercing eyes, intensely focused on the task at hand.

I asked an attractive, brown-haired woman dressed in a flowing purple outfit how she came to be here. "I was browsing in the bookstore, and the book literally fell on my head." She giggled. "I figured that it was a sign I should read it."

I met an older man who had greying hair and told me that he was a medical doctor interested in alternative healing. He said he could already perceive the energy field and wanted to be with a teacher who could confirm his perceptions. There was a veterinarian who wanted to learn hands-on healing for his animal clients. A few people had serious illnesses and had come to receive their own healing. There were yoga teachers, nurses, housewives, and homeopaths. I noticed that most of the attendees seemed older than me and already established in helping professions. I wondered what I had gotten myself into.

As the class began, the soft sound of harp music, played by student/assistant Marjorie Valerie, led us into a deep meditation. After a period of silence, Barbara stood up on the stage platform and welcomed us.

The first thing Barbara told us was to "fasten your seat belts!" During her introduction, she explained that energy healing wasn't simply a skill you did or did not have but that it was entirely teachable. Furthermore, she expanded on the ideas in her book, explaining how the energy body was a template for the physical body and that we could attune our consciousness to specific energetic frequencies to influence the physical body, provided that we could learn to hold these higher healing frequencies and transmit them through our hands. She explained that as we opened to higher frequencies, our own energy blocks would come up to be healed. This was the work of self-transformation.

She looked at all our eager faces and concluded with, "Healers, first heal thyself!" a phrase I recognized as coming from Jesus and later adopted by physicians. So an incredible weekend commenced, and I found myself stretched to capacity in ways I had never before experienced.

Opening to Subtle Reality

During one exercise, we explored psychometry, the art of sensing the energies embedded in physical objects. We broke up into dyads (pairs) and exchanged a personal object with our partner.

I received a ring that my partner took off her finger and handed to me. As I held it in my hand, I tried to clear my thoughts and simply feel through the physicality of the ring for any vibrations, images, or feelings that might be there. At first, nothing happened, but then I felt a vague sense of a grandmother's presence and sadness. Not an earth-shattering reading; however, it was accurate. The grandmother had died a few years back, and the stone in the ring had been hers.

We learned a basic healing technique called a chelation, transmitting energy from our hands to a "client," starting at the feet, then up the legs, to the sixth chakra. Barbara taught that there are seven major chakras (the word "chakra" means "wheel of light" in Sanskrit) in the energy body. We never transmitted energy to what she called the seventh chakra. I later learned that the correct term for the "seventh" chakra is Sahasrara, or the Thousand-Petaled Lotus. In yogic texts, it is not considered a chakra; rather it is the gateway to God consciousness, pictured as a lotus blossom with one thousand petals, the opening of which symbolizes illumination and enlightenment.

The first time I paired up as healer with a fellow student, I had no clue what I was doing. I just followed the instructions, imagining the energy flowing through my hands as I moved them to each body location. I could vaguely sense some heat and movement under my hands, and my client seemed to relax and breathe more fully. As my hands moved up the body, I became incredibly hot, to the point that sweat dripped off my face. I felt completely exhausted afterward. I couldn't imagine doing more than four of these a day as a professional healer.

Afterward, Barbara explained that each of us already had a preferred high-sense mechanism that we used all the time in our daily lives. These four modes of perception are:

- *Kinesthetic sense*, when you feel and receive information through physical touch.

- *Clairvoyance*, when you use the visual sense to see images on your mind screen or see into the body as if you have X-ray vision.

- *Clairaudience*, when you use the auditory sense to hear subtle sound or guidance as if someone is speaking to you.

- *Clairsentience*, when you have an inner sense of things, manifesting in a strong knowing or intuition.

She mentioned that there is even a high-sense perception of smell, which is when different types of scents, like the smell of certain flowers or the smell of death, give you information. Barbara assured us that during our training, we would learn to develop whatever our natural primary sense was, as well as improve our other, less-used senses.

When I started the healing training, I primarily used my kinesthetic sense. This surprised me, because as an artist, I was so visual. Echoing what Lady Diana had said, I discovered that my hands often knew where to go on someone's body without consulting my mind.

As a child, I had always heard an inner voice who I assumed was my imaginary friend. I would often talk to it and rehearse the questions I would ask my mother later. As I opened up in the training, I recognized that voice as a form of guidance from my higher self that intensified when I did energy healings. I would hear the voice internally as it told me where to put my hands and when to move them. The more I accepted this guidance, the more clearly I would receive information.

One doesn't need to be a channel of disincarnate beings to receive guidance; we all have access to this inner voice. The voice always conveyed higher wisdom and values, and with practice I was able to distinguish it from my own personal desires. Often, I would check the information it provided three times before acting on it. If the guidance remained the same, I would follow its counsel. Sometimes the inner voice provided information, such as about the client's ancestors, that I had no way of knowing. As I developed the courage to share this information with my clients, they would usually verify its accuracy.

My own High Sense Perception (HSP) developed gradually during years of practice. As I trusted the clairaudience and kinesthetic senses, the clairvoyance and clairsentience modes became more active. Today, when I do energy healings, the exact amount of information needed in the moment comes through—I sense, see, hear, or know it. But back then, it didn't seem possible that I could learn to perceive in this way.

Barbara demonstrated healing techniques throughout the weekend, and even though I couldn't "see" the energy field, my narrower view of reality rubbed up against her expanded view of reality, and little windows of perception popped open. I would sense something briefly in the way that you catch a movement from the corner of your eye; it went by too fast to name, but nevertheless it appeared. When Barbara named it, I could recognize it the next time around. Her confirmation and validation were what allowed me to open to a wider perception of the subtle world.

Toward the end of the weekend, Barbara asked for a volunteer client for a healing demonstration. A young woman raised her hand; she complained that she felt like she was dying. She had no appetite, no affect in her voice, a pale complexion, lifeless hair, and a host of unrelated medical symptoms for which her doctor could find no cause. This woman lived in New York but had spent time in Jamaica with a boyfriend with whom she was no longer involved.

Barbara did a long healing on her. At times, I watched her breathe rapidly as her hands moved in the air, interacting with forces that I couldn't perceive. At other times, she was completely silent and still. At one point, she asked the woman if she was ready to permanently disconnect from the boyfriend. The woman answered yes. At the end of the healing, the whole room felt permeated with a golden light. It was so palpable that we all basked in a state of deep silence and peace.

Barbara explained later that she had done a kind of exorcism on the woman, removing a curse put on her by the boyfriend, who had hired a black magician.

Hearing that, a ripple of fear ran through my body, and I questioned whether I wanted to do this kind of work after all. The description of black magic and exorcism were so way out of the realm of what I thought was real and acceptable that I wondered if my parents had been right. What was I getting into?

However, Barbara then shared that she used an advanced healing technique called the Core Star healing, which we would learn in our fourth year; this healing engaged the Core Star in the center of her body, the unique individual God center within each person. By expanding her Core Essence, the curse was removed.

The woman looked visibly different after the healing; she had flushed cheeks and warmth in her eyes. More life force animated her body, and there was a vitality that clearly hadn't been there when the healing started.

By chance, I ran into her on the Upper West Side some months later and asked her how she was doing. She told me that after the healing, all her symptoms had disappeared, her desire to live had come back immediately, and she has been well ever since.

This served as a good confirmation for me, as I had just enrolled in the Barbara Brennan School of Healing (BBSH) four-year program.

3

Healing School Begins

East Hampton, New York, 1988

If the doors of perception were cleansed every thing would appear to man as it is: Infinite.

—Walt Whitman

One hundred twenty-six of us gathered in Bridgehampton, New York, for this first large-scale training in healing science. Before this year, Barbara had taught only a few small groups of students. This group hailed from all over the United States. A few people even came from Europe. Amongst us were doctors, nurses, chiropractors, housewives, physical therapists, psychologists, and veterinarians.

I was one of the youngest in the group and had no previous experience with energy work, touching bodies, or psychotherapy. I embarked on this quest for transformation with uncontainable excitement, unable to imagine the end point of the journey that would culminate in opening a healing practice of my own. I showed up at every class with a sense of wonder and discovery.

The community room, set up with rows of folding tables topped with soft pads and blankets, looked like a makeshift triage center. We paired up, student healer with student client, to practice the steps of a chelation, the hands-on healing that we had learned in the introductory workshop. We were guided to start by holding our client's feet and gradually work our way up the body, touching the ankles, knees, hips, and six of the chakras.

I imagined light coming from my hands and charging each chakra with energy. An assistant standing on the stage said, "Just allow the energy to flow outward from your hands. Don't push or pull; stay in allow mode."

I had never done anything remotely like this, and touching someone in this way felt very unfamiliar. To my surprise, my hands became very warm, heating up as soon as they made contact with the woman lying on my healing table. My hands could sense the energy flowing upward through her body, a movement that was subtle but palpable. Halfway into the healing, I became very tired. My back hurt and my energy waned.

I could hear other people on the tables crying, moaning, and screaming. It made me anxious. I wondered if I had landed in an otherworldly hospital or a loony bin.

As Barbara Brennan glided over to my table to check my technique, she fixed her laser beam eyes on me, and I could feel her gaze tickle my insides as it scoured my innermost being. The air around us thickened and seemed electrified.

"Dani, you need more energy to do this work. Try breathing like this," she suggested. She expelled air forcefully through her nose, a technique that brings light and oxygen into the pituitary gland in the center of the brain. She told me that it would increase my ability to see different levels of reality by opening the sixth chakra.

I bravely imitated her breathing, making snorting noises through my nose. I became a little light-headed.

"You need more grounding; feel your feet," Barbara said, noticing that I was about to swoon. "That's it, now just sink your energy hand in deeper there. Can you feel that? Dani, you are seeing!" she pronounced suddenly. "Can you see the green heart chakra under your hand?"

Just as she spoke, I could see it: a small, emerald-green heart chakra, spinning like a top. It appeared on my mind screen, visible with my eyes closed, like a dream image.

Within seconds the image began to fade. Barbara noticed and instructed, "Feel your legs and draw energy up through the earth. You need more power. Then allow the energy to come out of your hands."

I bent my legs and imagined red-hot energy coming up from the core of the earth, through my legs, my torso, down my arms, and into my hands. I flushed and started sweating as a surge of energy transferred from my hands to my client, who registered the energy with a sigh as her whole body relaxed.

"Good," Barbara confirmed, as she moved on to assist the next healer.

What just happened? I wondered, elated that I could suddenly see a chakra.

The likely explanation is that Barbara's higher vibration induced in me the ability to see on the subtle level. It was as if a veil had lifted and the chakra simply appeared on my mind's screen. Although my eyes were closed, no effort was required to see it.

Most of us came to the school because we wanted Barbara's magical ability to see into the body and soul.

There is a deep power in being truly seen; it gives us the confidence to live into our true potential.

We explored subtle energy as if it were the most normal thing in the world. Being in the company of like-minded others created a group resonance, which facilitated faster learning of these skills. The energy work itself came easily to me. We practiced opening to the different levels of the energy field, very much like the way a vocalist practices musical scales.

Barbara, standing on the stage, would call out: "Feel your first chakra and the first level of your energy field; see the color red, make your hands the same vibration as the color red. Feel your second chakra and the second level of your energy field; see the color orange, and make your hands the same vibration as the color orange. . . ." and so on.

From the first to seventh levels, we practiced until we were proficient at keeping our consciousness focused, so that later we could learn specific healing techniques by holding the frequency and color of each level.

When I stood amongst my classmates doing these "energy scales," I could feel my hands matching the vibration of the group's energy. I could even tell when someone else wasn't holding the right frequency or color. It felt like a hole in the group field.

Once, I volunteered to have Barbara "read" me in front of the room.

She scanned my aura and pronounced: "Dani, everything is fine in your energy system; you are in homeostasis. However, you hold down all your emotions, and your physical body is so tight it doesn't get enough energy flow. Your third chakra compensates for this depletion by trying to suck energy from other people."

Who me, an energy vampire? I thought to myself.

She continued, "If you want to work on this, you are going to have to open up and inquire into your relationship with your mother."

I groaned inwardly—my mother!—a lot of fun that will be.

In my family, we didn't look too deeply into anything, whether interior or exterior. We were not a self-reflective bunch. When I mentioned to my parents that I had started therapy, they responded almost in unison: "Why stir anything up? What for? Leave everything alone, and it will go away."

I am sure they were afraid that I would criticize their job as parents. Also there was plenty they wanted to forget in their own lives.

But this deep journey inward was so much more than simply unearthing childhood wounds. At first, it felt like opening Pandora's box, as every facet of false self came out to assert its place. Witnessing and taking responsibility for my own unconscious actions initiated a complete review of all of my previously unexamined motives. Why did I react that way? Why do I feel threatened here or invaded there?

My lessons in energy healing quickened the process and supported new patterns of relating to myself and to others. We delved in to the psychodynamics of each chakra, enabling us to learn about and heal our own energy blocks. Psychotherapy gave me a context to understand my early childhood wounding. I began to realize that as much as my mother loved me, I grew up feeling deprived and needy.

As I addressed my nourishment issues, I went all the way back to infancy. As an infant, I'd had allergies to milk that weren't discovered until I had screamed my head off for a few months. As we heal, our biggest wounds turn into our greatest gifts. The ironic gift of healing this wound of being undernourished is that I now feel full enough to help nourish others.

Past-Life Healing

We spent quite a few sessions learning how to do past-life healings. I don't look at past lives as being in a linear past; although they sure seem to be when they are activated. When these deep patterns of our soul materialize, it feels as if all time is present at once. "Past" lives always connect to patterns/anxieties/fears in our current life. They appear in the energy field as dark spots of frozen energy. They dissolve as consciousness is brought to the frozen actions, emotions, and beliefs associated with them.

Lives with similar themes are stacked in nested layers within the subtle body, like an onion. When you are ready to address their themes, they present themselves for healing. The results of past-life healing can be profound as a conglomerate of symptoms resolve and limiting beliefs disappear.

Once, while sitting next to Barbara on the stage, I silently observed a student healer struggling with a writhing patient on the table. I somehow "knew" there was an astral remnant of a sword from a past life in the patient's heart.

Barbara confirmed my knowing by saying, "Dani, go over there and remove the sword from her heart. Then sew the wound and fill it with rose light."

I looked at Barbara, amazed again at her capacity to see. I would never have believed my inner knowing if she hadn't been there to validate it.

I went over to the healer, asked if I could help, and as I put my hands in the energy field I could feel the etheric sword. I could describe its size and shape, as if it had a solid form. As soon as I grasped it, there was a kind of resistance, and when I pulled it out, the patient stopped writhing and settled down.

My fingers flew rapidly in the air as they sewed the wounded area with lines of light that projected from my fingertips like a spider making his web. I then filled the area with rose light, the color of love.

Later, the client confirmed my perceptions by sharing her own vivid images of being stabbed in the heart in some long-ago past and how it felt in relation to a recent betrayal by her boyfriend. Her immediate confirmation gave me validation.

By the third year of training, we had volunteer clients of our own, and I started to receive supervision from more advanced healers in the training. We talked about the responsibilities of having a professional healing practice. Things were starting to get very real.

Although working on family members was not rec-ommended, during our training my dad had to have open-heart surgery. I offered him an energy healing after the surgery, and he gratefully consented because he was in so much pain.

When I arrived at his hospital room, he was only one day out of the ICU. I felt shocked when I saw my usually vibrant dad looking as if he had aged ten years in just twenty-four hours. His skin had a blue-grey tinge, and he looked so vulnerable and thin bundled up in the sheets. I stood at the foot of the bed and held his feet. I tried hard to come into a neutral space to do the healing, but

I just wanted to cry. I blocked out the hospital smells and noises, and took a few deep breaths to center myself.

As my hands moved up his body, my fingers could feel holes in the first level of his energy field, which looked like a web of electric-blue lines of light, following the form of his physical body. The first level of his field had a lot of torn and frayed blue lines that formed holes, like the holes in a mesh window screen, particularly near his heart and sternum. I repaired the holes by weaving lines of laser-blue light that came from my fingertips.

After I finished, my dad turned his head and said: "You touched every place where the doctors inserted tubes during the surgery. The pain is much less now, and I could feel what you were doing. Thanks, sweetie," he whispered, as he fell back asleep.

He never used the term "It's all bullshit" about the healing work again.

And I started to believe in my new role as a healer.

4

A Healing Crisis

New York, 1990

The most fundamental aggression to ourselves, the most fundamental harm we can do to ourselves, is to remain ignorant by not having the courage and the respect to look at ourselves honestly and gently.

—Pema Chödrön, *When Things Fall Apart*

The shell around my emotions finally cracked open.

During an exercise in which we were asked to scan our lower chakras, my body shook with pain and fear. I couldn't suppress screams as images of abuse at the hands of men paraded before my vision. It felt like my womb was being cut open. I cried and cried and cried. For a period of time, I couldn't bear to be touched.

Although I had never experienced sexual abuse in this lifetime, these sensory memories were vivid and violent. I went home from that class exhausted, and I hibernated in my bed, curled up under the covers. I became hypersensitive to any nuance of violence in the world, and I couldn't watch the news without bursting into tears.

When the crying period ended, massive, uncontainable rage arose. I wanted to kill everyone: the taxi drivers, my husband, my parents, and my friends. Issues that had been locked up in my first and second chakras were being purged. I realized that for most of my life I had functioned with an edge of indignant anger that seeped out in almost all of my interactions. If my immediate needs weren't met, I got irritable. Quickly. Even with waitresses and salespeople. I walked around in the belief that everyone was out to cheat or mistreat me. My mother operated like that, and I thought it was a normal.

Often I couldn't stop my angry reactions in the moment, but afterward I could observe myself and analyze what had triggered me. In therapy, I banged my fists into a pillow to make the anger conscious. Eventually, anger became my friend, and I didn't need to passively project it onto strangers. I could own it and express it directly. When a core belief system starts to dissolve, every level of your life either gets recalibrated or disintegrates. My friends changed and my marriage became strained.

Around this time, during a routine gynecology exam, I received a diagnosis of cervical dysplasia, a precancerous condition of cervical cells due to the human papilloma virus (HPV).

In regards to my physical condition, my doctor advised me to have laser treatments to burn off the abnormal cells. After two or three painful treatments, the abnormal cells were still growing.

"I am an energy healer," I declared to my doctor. "I want to get some healings and see if it makes a difference." It was the first time I had claimed my new profession. "I know a healer who can help me. Can I come back in six months to see if there are positive results from the healings?"

She was open-minded and agreed, saying: "It's a slow-growing condition, and we can monitor it carefully."

I had heard about the talents of Jason Shulman from my Barbara Brennan classmates. Rumor had it that he was Barbara's star student. He could *see* like she did, and after sessions with him, my friends would compare notes with each other. Jason himself had come to do healing work through his own search to cure undiagnosable symptoms that had disabled him for more than seven years.

One friend confided after a session with him: "He said my kidneys were weak, and I needed this homeopathic remedy. And then when I returned the next time, he told me exactly how much of the remedy was still in my energy field." Whispered accounts of his healing sessions created an aura of awe around him.

I had been curious about his talents but felt something had to be wrong with me before I could consult him. Now I had the chance. I felt scared when I phoned him to book some healing sessions, not knowing what to expect. Nervously, I repeated the doctor's diagnosis. "I have a precancerous condition of the cervix called dysplasia."

"Yes, yes, I can see exactly where the abnormal cells are; it won't be a problem to remove them. I have done this before. It will take a few sessions," he reassured me.

I felt a wave of relief flood my body, and I booked a series of healings with him.

I took a two-hour train ride from New York City to his home office in northern New Jersey. As I waited outside on the porch, I could hear the sounds of family life through the screen door. His dog was barking, his young daughter was running around, and his wife was in the kitchen. A perfectly normal suburban scenario.

He came outside and welcomed me in to his office. Jason was in his late forties, bearded, and had silvery white hair and the high, balding forehead of an ancient Jewish sage. "Sit opposite me so that I can scan your energy field," he said.

I plopped down on a rolling, black office chair opposite him. He asked me to slide back a bit, and he squinted his eyes as he scanned my energy field. He made a few "humpfs" and stroked his beard.

"Been angry lately?" he asked.

"Uh, yes," I mumbled.

"Underneath your rage I see a small, needy child, demanding proper nourishment and care," he said gently. "You need to take care of her through imaginative dialogue work. You should dialogue with the parts of her that are screaming to be heard. Maybe you could keep a journal," he suggested.

He then had me lie down on his massage table, fully clothed. He put a cloth over my pelvic area just so I would feel less vulnerable. He went over to a table where various crystals were arrayed and chose one that had a clear, pointed tip.

"You will probably feel this," he explained. "I am going to scrape the precancerous cells off your cervix with this crystal."

I closed my eyes and tried to relax. He slowly passed the crystal over the area of my body where the cervix would be located. I could immediately feel a scraping sensation, as if there were a surgical instrument deep inside me. It wasn't painful, but it was strangely physical. I could feel him removing something in there, even though his hand was above my body.

This "surgery" was finished in what felt like minutes, but actually a half hour had gone by. He filled and protected the whole area with light, and I drifted into a relaxed and altered state of consciousness. When I got off the table I felt light-headed.

"I think you should see my homeopath in New York," he recommended. "Homeopathy will support your body's healing process." He gave me some water to drink and told me I could sit outside on his porch until I felt ready to go back to the train station for the ride home.

I had three sessions with him before I went back to my doctor. I also saw the homeopath he had recommended and took two homeopathic remedies over a six-month period. I will never forget the look on my doctor's face when she finished her exam.

She remarked with amazement: "Well, I have never seen such a positive result without surgery. Keep doing what you are doing and come back again in six months."

Six months later, the abnormal cells had completely disappeared.

My doctor said: "You know, sometimes these things clear up by themselves." She had to make the point that there was no scientific proof that the healings and homeopathy were what cured me.

I, however, felt a shift after every healing. I know this condition didn't disappear by itself. The homeopathy helped stabilize the energy work. Every year afterward when I saw the doctor for my exam, she never failed to tell me that my results were remarkable. Nevertheless, my doubt about the effectiveness of energy healing work continued to be my companion.

Marjorie Valerie, one of Barbara's senior students, accompanied all our class sessions with her improvised harp music. A raven-haired beauty, she sat to Barbara's right on stage. She had an arresting presence, like a dark-haired Dolly Parton, with her milky-white skin and voluptuous body. In my memory, her music is forever intertwined with the process of doing a healing.

When she played, it felt as if a host of angels swooped in to surround our tables with celestial comfort. Her fingers plucked sweeping arpeggios, the notes rising faster and faster, lifting us to celestial levels. She mentored me and helped me bridge the growing chasm between my life at home and the one at school. She had become my personal friend after she had played the harp as I walked down the aisle at my wedding.

I felt shocked when she confided in me that she was battling breast cancer. The disbelief and shock about her diagnosis quickly spread through the entire community. All of us had the same unspoken questions: How could someone so close to Barbara have cancer? Barbara will cure her, won't she? Does this energy healing really work?

Sadly, Marjorie did not live, despite the fact that she had a great doctor, did every treatment Western medicine could offer, and had many healings. I struggled to understand how someone as beautiful and talented as she, someone in the prime of her life who had so much to give to the world, could die. It brought up the deepest of questions: Why do some people heal and others die? What is the difference between healing and curing? Is this work real?

5

My Marriage Falls Apart

New York, 1990s

Barbara warned us as we left each class: "You are in an expanded state of consciousness. Be gentle with yourselves when you go home. At some point this expansion becomes stasis and then you can expect a contraction. Don't think you are going backward. Don't push yourself out of one stage into the next. Allow yourself to ride the wave and complete each stage as you integrate your experiences."

My normal life seemed mundane and monotonous in comparison to the stratospheric atmosphere of the training, where everything was heightened and miraculous. However, in the weeks after class, I welcomed the structure of my daily life as a time to reflect on everything that had happened. Which was the dream world and which was the real world? I wondered.

At the trainings, I had the luxury of uninterrupted time to focus on inner work with a community of people devoted to self-transformation. Experiencing the open, emotional authenticity of my classmates made me long for that level of deep contact in other areas of my life.

Inevitably, on my first night home from class, during dinner, I wanted to share my experiences with my husband Reuben. "Guess what we did at school this week, honey? We learned sound healing and sang tones into a woman's liver to heal her from parasites."

Even though I knew beforehand that he couldn't relate to a thing I said, I plunged onward. "Then we practiced past-life healing. One of my friends relived the birth of five stillborn children. She was screaming at the top of her lungs, as if they were being born right in the room. Three healers had to be her midwives and hold her as she grieved the loss of those children."

Reuben, eyes glazed, managed to nod politely with a "yes, dear" look, the equivalent to "you've gotta be kidding, right?" He tried to hear my experiences with an open mind, but we grew further and further apart as I went through the training. Eventually, I didn't confide in him until after two days had passed, and I had started to contract from the expanded state. I did not yet have the maturity to be more relational and to temper my comments so that he could hear them.

On the outside, we continued to appear to be the perfect couple, but increasingly our marriage felt like a façade. Perhaps our disastrous honeymoon indicated our marriage had been doomed from the start.

Three months after our wedding, we had embarked on an eight-week honeymoon to some of the most spectacular cities in Italy and southern France. During our first week in Florence, we found ourselves standing in front of a beautiful storefront that said something like "Tea and Tarot Readings" in Italian, French, and English.

"Let's get readings!" I said, and Reuben didn't object.

A bell jingled as we opened the door, and our eyes adjusted to the dim light as we entered the room. Like a perfectly decorated stage set, brass lanterns were scattered through the room, a kilim-covered couch sat against the wall, and tiled floors peeked out from below scattered throw rugs.

A tall, dark-haired, Moroccan man emerged from a back room and asked us in French-accented English, "What would you like?"

"We'd like to have tarot readings," I said.

He gazed at us solemnly and replied: "Come back in an hour, and I will have time for both of you."

An hour later, he beckoned Reuben in first. I went out to take a neighborhood walk. I found myself drawn into a Florentine paper shop to pick out ornate stationery for my mother and sister back home. I returned to the storefront just as Reuben emerged from the back room.

"How was your reading?" I asked.

"It was amazing!" Reuben exclaimed. "He really got me."

Great! I thought to myself, excited to hear what the reader would say to me. I loved tarot and had studied it myself for over a year.

I followed the tarot reader into the back room and sat on some cushions. He handed me an old, worn tarot deck, and I shuffled the cards. I picked out several cards and carefully placed them in the order he suggested. He was silent for a moment.

Then he looked me straight in the eyes and said: "Why are you married to this man? You shouldn't be married to anyone. You don't need a man, and marriage is not your purpose in this life. This marriage won't last."

He wasn't even reading the cards. He may have said other things, but my mind was so stunned, I froze. I could see his mouth moving, but I couldn't hear a thing. When he finished, I gathered my purse and jacket and left the back room to rejoin Reuben.

Reuben suggested that we wait to share our readings with each other over a picnic dinner. I tried to compose myself as we picked up fresh bread, cheese, olives, and wine and went to a plaza overlooking all of Florence.

I couldn't eat.

"He told me I shouldn't be married to you," I blurted out.

There was a deathly silence. "It's true," Reuben sobbed softly, not meeting my eyes. "I don't know if I want to be married."

I squeaked out: "What do you mean? We've been married all of three months! You're bailing out now?"

I couldn't believe what I was hearing; our future crumbled before my eyes. We both came from families in which marriage was supposed to be forever. I couldn't imagine my parents' reaction if we admitted failure after only three months.

By this time, I was in total shock. How could this be happening to me—on my honeymoon?

I did not see myself as someone who made decisions based on psychic readings, channeled, tarot, or otherwise. Yet my healing career had started with a channeled reading and my marriage seemed to be ending because of a tarot reading! This sounded like a new age soap opera even to me.

I felt flooded with shame and despair. I never expected Reuben to confirm the reading. I had hoped he would laugh it off and tell me it was all new age nonsense, and that he didn't believe in this kind of stuff anyway. We had just started our trip, and we continued onward through the dazzling beauty of Positano, Capri, Tuscany, Cannes, and Monaco. I couldn't recalibrate. Dazed, my dreams were shattered, and my heart felt heavy with disappointment.

I imagine every marriage goes through a shattering when you stop idealizing your partner and realize that you have to accept their imperfections. However, for most people, this is where the true journey of marriage and intimacy begins. Sadly, this wouldn't be the case for us.

This incident did open a deeper level of honesty and communication than we'd ever had before, and by the end of our honeymoon we'd made a resolution to work on our relationship. We entered couples' therapy as soon as we returned to New York City.

Of course, the first thing any therapist asks is, "How did you two meet?" to remind you of the initial spark that attracted you to your partner.

I struggled to tell this story with delight as if it were still apparent that we were meant to be together. But our honeymoon had cast a dark shadow over my heart.

From the beginning, we'd had a deep friendship, but we'd interacted more like brother and sister than boyfriend and girlfriend; something that should have led me to a different evaluation of our strengths as potential husband and wife. At some essential level, we loved each other; however, I didn't have that automatic lighting up inside when he entered a room or that feeling of adoration.

Reuben had a tendency toward depression, which I am sure carried over from his parents' experiences during the war. Often the children of survivors inherit all the unprocessed feelings of their parents. All of my aliveness and excitement must have both attracted and threatened him.

I often felt lonelier in my marriage than I had when I had been single. I wanted deep contact. I wanted passionate sex. I wanted to explore my anger and wanted someone who could meet me emotionally. I would reach out to touch him, and he would close down and curl away from me. He would feel my neediness and want to flee.

With my expanded energies beginning to cause more of a chasm in our marriage, we made an effort to grow closer by attending a couples' communication workshop at Kripalu Yoga Center in Massachusetts.

A former Jesuit monastery, Kripalu was spare in décor but imbued with an atmosphere of silence and discipline. Pictures of the guru, Amrit Desai, were everywhere. We fell into the rhythm of ashram life and vegetarian food, a new experience for both of us.

I had never seen a "yogi," but I knew that in Judaism each person had their own direct connection to God that needed no intermediary. Worshipping a person as the incarnation of the Divine was forbidden, hence the problem with Jesus. Here, people bowed to the guru with great reverence, and we both felt uncomfortable with the adoration. Fortunately, he was not in residence the weekend we were there.

For three days, we stared deeply into each other's eyes and practiced clear, nonblaming communication.

I feel _____ when you do _____ and would like it if you did _____. Are you willing to try that?

We squirmed as we took turns expressing our feelings and listening to each other in this stilted manner.

As squirmy and contrived as it seemed at the time, it did create some ease and intimacy.

I didn't know then that the founder, Yogi Amrit Desai, had experienced some kind of Kundalini arousal, the awakening of the feminine spiritual force within, which begins the journey of spiritual life. In his case, when Kundalini awakened, he experienced an involuntary and spontaneous flow of yoga postures that flowed seamlessly through his body. He later named this type of flowing yoga *Kripalu yoga* after his own guru in India, Swami Kripalu.

I also could not have imagined that Yogic Science would eventually become such a prominent part of my own spiritual practice. At that time, yoga studios were not yet as common as the neighborhood gym, and trained yoga teachers were not readily available. At the Barbara Brennan School of Healing, we had never studied the original Vedic and Tantric texts, which are the repository for the tradition's precise knowledge of the chakras.

The more I stared at the pictures of Gurudev—beloved guru, as he was affectionately called—the more my curiosity was piqued. What made people so attracted to him that they would leave their homes and live in an ashram in such an ascetic manner? What would it mean to have a spiritual teacher? Why did his students bow to him? He seemed to be worshipped as an incarnation of God.

All these questions swirled in my mind as I walked the serene halls of Kripalu for the last time. With a poignant sadness, we packed our bags in preparation to leave. I had gotten accustomed to the silence, the daily yoga, and the vegetarian meals.

As we waited for the bus to take us back to New York, we promised each other we would make weekly appointments to practice our communication skills. Of course, that promise didn't keep beyond our first weeks home. I believe we both knew that the workshop would not save our marriage.

As we boarded, Reuben handed the driver our tickets. In the moment he withdrew his hand, his wedding band flew off his finger. Startled, we looked at each other. The truth of what that meant did not need to be spoken.

6

Seduced by a Dark Guide

New York, 1992-1995

Whatever is rejected from the self, appears in the world as an event.

—Carl Jung

After our Kripalu experience, I devoured the book *Autobiography of a Yogi*, by Paramahansa Yogananda, to better understand yogis and the yogic tradition. I was enthralled by Yogananda's faith in God and his encounters with saints and realized beings, and the book awakened in me a profound desire for a spiritual teacher.

One night, our local yoga teacher invited us to attend a gathering at which a female friend of his would be hosting a French man who claimed to be a spiritual teacher, yogi, and healer. Conveniently, she held the meeting in her apartment right across the street from where we lived.

Reuben and I walked into her dimly lit living room where a beautiful man in crisp yogic whites sat perched atop a meditation cushion. His long, dark hair was flecked with grey and artfully fanned out over the wool meditation shawl covering his shoulders. He looked like the perfect combination of an older Jesus and a modern yogi.

He called himself Sananda, which means joy or delight in Sanskrit. Sananda was appearing in my life as I finished my last year of training at the Barbara Brennan School. His intent was to come to the United States over a period of three years to teach us his method of healing.

He surveyed the room, his intelligent blue-grey eyes taking us in with a look of amusement. He spoke only French, and a translator conveyed his words to us. A Francophile at heart, I could understand most of what he said directly, having had at least three French boyfriends, two French bosses, and many years of French lessons at the renowned Alliance Français in New York City.

"I work as a cosmic garbage collector. I am here to wield Saint Michael's sword, to cut through your karma and collect all of your past garbage, so that you can be free," Sananda said with utter belief in himself.

He spoke of his love of Jesus as if he had been a disciple.

"Jesus was the real healer. He surrendered his life to God. It is God who heals. I am not the healer, you are not the healer—that would be ego. I will teach you how to get your ego out of the way and let the real healer heal. I will help you become clear of your past."

Though soft-spoken, his words had a magnetic power to them, and a palpable energy spread through the room like thick honey. I should have felt alarmed by the aggrandizement coming through his speech, but instead I felt swept up in his love of God and the confidence he exuded; he seemed so sure of his ability to guide people spiritually. For me it was love at first sight.

I was a novice to gurus and spiritual teachers. I didn't know the importance of knowing your teacher's lineage; in other words, your teacher's teachers. Sananda vaguely alluded to meeting with a yogi in India from time to time, but we never got the sense that he had to answer to anyone else other than himself and God. I realize only now, with the benefit of hindsight, how naïve I was.

And so started the most cringe-worthy episode of my nascent spiritual life.

After Sananda's introductory talk, we were invited to approach him individually to ask a personal question. I spoke to him directly in my college French.

"A few months ago, I had an inexplicable experience while I was sleeping. Can you explain it?"

He nodded for me to continue.

"One night, I came home from my energy healing retreat and went to sleep alone, because Reuben was out of town. I retired early, exhausted from the week at class.

"I had a frightening dream. I remember seeing a metal box that was emitting light, and I heard a roaring noise. I woke up from the dream and there was electricity going up and down my spine, and I could still hear the loud noise. I couldn't move my arms or legs. I was paralyzed. I felt terrified, as if someone or something were pinning me down. I dozed off again, and I found myself in an astral, hell-like realm where I zapped horrible-looking creatures with the light coming from my hands."

Sananda didn't respond for a while. He then simply said it was a spiritual experience to help me open up my energy body.

His answer came closest to the truth. Of the other teachers I had asked before him, one had said it was extraterrestrials, which did nothing to alleviate my fear, and another had said it was an initiation. But Sananda's answer resonated with me, and I was intrigued to see what else he could teach me.

Captivated by his charisma, I convinced Reuben to attend the introductory weekend held in the same apartment across the street, and we then signed up for his intensive training program. Everyone brought sleeping bags and stayed overnight so that Sananda could work on our energy bodies while we slept.

The weekend was powerful, with many meditations that left me swooning in a state of ecstasy. On the last day of the weekend, we each had a private exit interview with him. I came into the room and sat cross-legged opposite him.

"Come closer," he said. I moved in toward him till our knees were touching. He pressed his thumb into my third eye, and my whole body shook rapidly as light spiraled up my spine.

Then he chanted the *bija* mantras in Sanskrit, which are the seed syllables for each chakra. "Lam, Vam, Ram, Ham, Yam, Om . . ."

More intense light spiraled up my spine, exploding in my head.

I opened my eyes and stared into his. Then he leaned over and kissed me on my lips.

I was shocked. And also flattered. I just sat there, not knowing what to do. Then he told me to leave the room.

My husband, sitting in the living room with the others, glanced up at me as I entered. I couldn't look him in the eye, and I didn't tell anyone what had happened. If only I'd had the sense to walk away right then and there.

Ignoring all these warning signs, I fell in love with him spiritually and surrendered myself inwardly to his care. He was the most powerful and seductive man I have ever met, and he started coming to me astrally at night as I lay next to my husband. I recognized his bodiless presence by a palpable golden light hovering over the bed. Then it felt like he merged with me, soul to soul, and infused me with the most delicious sexually charged energy.

It's difficult to explain how I knew it was Sananda who came to me in his astral form, but it felt similar to how you recognize someone you know in a dream. You just know it. It created an obsession, an addiction, and a constant longing for more of this potent elixir. I thought I was special, chosen, until I later found out that there were many women in his various groups that described the exact same astral seduction.

My spiritual ego got more and more inflated, fed by his attention and recognition. I could soar higher and higher into spiritual states in his presence. I became an energy junkie, learning how to navigate and identify different spiritual realms with ease. Sometimes the energy was so intense that it felt as if the bones in my head moved to accommodate the electrical force. I didn't know then that spiritual experiences, while wonderful, are not necessarily a sign of real spiritual progress. And I knew nothing at the time about Kundalini, so I attributed all the fireworks to him.

He never made any other overtly sexual moves toward me, but he continued to stoke my burning energy system by directing transmissions of energy into my Ajna chakra. He did this with everyone, as if he were giving *shaktipat* (a transmission of energy from a guru).

Reuben and I completed Sananda's Light Therapy training together. The main healing technique he taught consisted of hand movements over each chakra, as well as the joints, while reciting the Our Father and the Hail Mary. You can imagine the power of Sananda's charisma to get two Jews to be receptive to this Christian-based technique!

Toward the end of our marriage, Reuben and I spent a month apart. I went to Southern France to attend a ten-day retreat with Sananda; Reuben traveled around Europe by himself. We met up afterward in France, and just like our honeymoon five years earlier, we were miserable together. Our marriage was clearly over.

Months after we separated, I invited Sananda to my new apartment, and he came to spend the day with me. I couldn't sleep the night before in anticipation of his visit. I polished my nails red and carefully chose my outfit for the next day, right down to the sexy underwear.

After years of tantalizing astral contact, I couldn't believe that I would finally be alone with him—in the physical. He arrived by taxi, and when I opened the door I was surprised to see him in normal clothes. He looked less powerful, smaller, more human and vulnerable.

He sat down on my sofa. "Would you like something to drink?" I asked in French.

"Yes, some tea, please," he said.

The reality of holding up my part of the conversation in French began to sink in as I struggled to express myself. At one point, I simply leaned in and kissed him on the lips.

He neither stopped me nor encouraged me, which confused me.

"Why don't you give me a healing? My back hurts and I am exhausted," he said.

I unfolded my healing table, and he lay down on his back. I started to channel energy through my hands through his feet. I couldn't believe I was touching him. By the time I got to his upper body, he pulled me on top of him. I tangled my fingers in his long hair as he stroked my back and pressed my spine in a certain spot that caused waves of ecstasy to flow through my body. It felt orgasmic without the sex.

We eventually made love, and I felt completely unified in heart, mind, and body. It felt surreal, and I had no thought of the future. Afterward, we dressed and walked all the way across Central Park to visit a sick friend of mine in the end stages of cancer. Sananda did some healing work with her and showed her great kindness and compassion.

We came back to my place and made love again. Lying together afterward, he rubbed the top of my head, and I floated upward, slipping out of my body into a bodiless bliss, high as a kite. We rested a while, then he dressed and called a cab to return to the house where he was staying. Once he'd left, I curled up under the blankets, inhaling the pungent smell of the essential oils he wore that had permeated the sheets.

I didn't hear from him for a few days. Then he called, and before I could even greet him, he said: "What happened between us will not happen again. I allowed it because of your love for me, but I am not the man for you. There is no relationship possible here. You will find someone else. I don't know when that will happen, but it will. You cannot be attached to me." He hung up the phone.

I froze in disbelief. I don't remember if I said anything in response before he hung up, but afterward, I got furious! He "allowed" it to happen?!! The nerve of him!

He was so cold and matter of fact. My heart shattered. I started wailing like a wounded animal. Two days later, he sent me a very nasty letter accusing me of judging him and abusing his kindness. I have no idea why he was so angry. I soon found out he was already seducing someone else in the group.

I had known all along that he was a womanizer, but I had felt so overwhelmed with lust that I would have done anything to sleep with him. My own blindness wouldn't allow me to see the truth till I got close enough to get hurt. However, that didn't excuse him from being a predator of the worst kind, one who presumes to teach spiritual truths and abuses the very real power he has and uses it for seduction.

His whole American group dissipated after word of this incident with me got out. I felt humiliated, brokenhearted, and ashamed.

Sananda seduced women in all of his groups and left a trail of broken hearts, taking advantage of his charisma and power for his own personal gains. I wish I could say that this was an uncommon occurrence in spiritual circles, but unfortunately it is not. What I did learn from this painful lesson was to be mindful of those I chose as my teachers—even those who claimed enlightenment.

A Jewish Divorce

Two weeks later, I met with Reuben in the office of a synagogue to arrange for a *get*, a Jewish document of divorce. Reuben wanted one in case he remarried someone religious, who would ask for it as proof that our divorce was final in the eyes of the Orthodox Jewish religion.

We entered an office and faced three white-haired and bearded rabbis sitting at a table. They asked us questions about our lineage, family names, and property distribution. One of them acted as the scribe and recorded our answers in Hebrew on thick paper scored with lines. He then folded the paper in a precise manner and had Reuben drop it into my hands.

As the paper softly landed in my open palms, I looked at Reuben and saw the same poignant sadness that washed through me mirrored in his eyes. I choked up as I left the room, walked down the hall, then returned. This walking away symbolized my leaving the marriage. Energetically, the bond between us as husband and wife broke in that moment. We said goodbye on the street corner and went our separate ways.

Facing My Shadow and Getting Free

I found a spiritually oriented therapist and started the work of grieving my marriage and the repair of my heart. I had to squarely face my shadow. I had to acknowledge how I had created and sustained the dynamic with Sananda. I had to face the part of myself that was so hungry for attention, to be seen and to feel special, especially in my marriage. Then I had to address my own lack of self-esteem and my need for validation.

In therapy, I allowed myself to feel the "Sananda" within me. I pictured myself as a teacher with great charisma and spiritual force, basking in the adoration of my students. I had a tiny drop of empathy for him as I imagined how enticed I would feel having all that adoration coming toward me. I knew that the same drive for seduction had fueled many of my own relationships with men. However, doing my own inner work didn't let him off the hook. He didn't hold his boundaries with integrity.

It is common knowledge today that many spiritual teachers and some of the yogis who have come to the West as renowned Swamis have succumbed to the lure of sexual relations with their students. A few years after my visit to Kripalu, I heard that the guru, Amrit Desai, had been thrown out of his own ashram by the residents for sexual misconduct. The list of fallen teachers is public knowledge and quite long.

In her book *Eyes Wide Open*, Mariana Caplan talks about the mutual complicity that can arise between the student and teacher that "unconsciously supports a distorted psychological dynamic between them"—a dangerous trap of unprocessed transference that many teachers and students fall into.

I was told by a male friend and fellow student of Sananda's that he had lovingly confronted Sananda on his seduction of women, and Sananda was unable to reflect on his actions in a responsible way. All he could say in response was: "I can't stop myself." He had no capacity to look at his own shadow. Since his relationships with female students were always consensual, there wasn't a way to prove abuse.

In the years since, a number of young women have come to me for help with similar experiences across all spiritual paths. I feel that I can assist them as they process their sense of betrayal and disillusionment and work with the idealized transference.

This type of spiritual abuse and disillusionment can either be a very fertile beginning for a real spiritual path— one that encourages the work of self-inquiry, purification of the ego, and psychological maturity—or it can be so devastating that the person shuts down spiritually for the remainder of their life. Somehow, my desire for God and the work of therapy helped me to choose spiritual maturity and use this experience to further my growth. I was fortunate to find some compassionate and nonjudgmental helpers.

Even after months of therapy, I still felt energetically connected to Sananda, as if I had given him my soul. At times, I felt energetically attacked by him. Despite receiving many healings, I couldn't release him from my body or energy field, and I felt slimy and invaded.

I decided to visit Mother Meera, an Indian woman who claims to be an incarnation of the Divine Mother, in Germany. She receives hundreds of people every evening at her home in the small town of Thalheim for a silent *darshan* (spiritual meeting with a saint or high being).

I stood outside her house in a quiet residential neighborhood with a couple hundred people. We entered in silence and awaited her presence. At 7:00 p.m. on the dot, she entered wearing a beautiful red and gold sari, eyes cast down. She looked to be in her late thirties, and the aura of light around her extended into the room as she walked directly toward her chair.

She sat down and with a nod of her head welcomed the first person to come before her, kneel down, and put their head in her hands. She gazed down as she did her silent work, clearing energetic knots along the person's spine that only she could perceive. Then she removed her hands and gazed deeply into the person's eyes to search their soul for places where she could help the person to have more freedom. All of this lasted around a minute, then the next person in line came forth.

When my turn to approach came, I felt naked in front of her as I silently begged for her help in releasing my soul from Sananda's grip. I felt an impersonal compassion in her gaze as I looked into her eyes. Then my minute before her was up, and I returned to my seat to meditate. She continued until all two hundred people had approached her; then she rose and silently left the room.

I had two dreams that week in Germany that finally released me.

In the first dream, I went to Mother Meera's home and asked her for help. She had me lie down on the floor and proceeded to pull thick, slimy, black cords from my hands, arms, feet, and legs. When she finished, she told me to go home, and I promptly woke up.

In the second dream, I confronted a metallic monster. I knew the monster was Sananda. I had to take my power back from him by grabbing three vials of essential oils that were placed at his feet. I approached him warily, grabbed the bottles, and ran.

As I analyzed the dream, I realized that the three vials represented the three levels of power that I had given away: physical, emotional, and spiritual. I needed to take back my desire to be seen by him, to have my light validated by him, and I had to start owning my own light and my own power. I had learned much about my devotional capacity through him, but I now knew my devotion needed to be directed toward God, not a teacher.

After the dreams, the astral attacks ceased, and I felt completely freed from any negative contact with him.

Part II

Kabbalah

The Jewish Mystical Path

7

A Society of Souls

Princeton, New Jersey, 1993

Everything that is allowed to exist, exists in light.

—Jason Shulman

I had been a Barbara Brennan graduate for just over a year and had a burgeoning healing practice in New York City when I received an announcement from Jason Shulman, the healer who had helped me cure my cervical dysplasia. He was starting his own school, a healing training rooted in Kabbalah, the Jewish mystical tradition.

The word *Kabbalah* means "to receive" in Hebrew. It represents the receiving of the deepest wisdom teachings within the Jewish mystical tradition. Like many secular Jews, I didn't know my religion contained within it a spiritual path. I felt intrigued and excited at the prospect of learning more about the often hidden and cryptic mystical tradition called Kabbalah at the heart of my own religion.

Even though I was wary of spiritual teachers after my experience with Sananda, my spiritual yearning overrode my doubts. More importantly for me, Jason was happily married and not seductive. I already knew him well as my healing supervisor. He seemed to know how to know God, and that spoke to the deep longing in my heart to be on a spiritual path.

I registered for his training, even though I had just opened my healing practice in New York City.

On our first day of class, we gathered in a mundane conference room in the Radisson Hotel on the outskirts of Princeton, New Jersey—an unlikely setting for the sacred material we were about to learn. Jason sat in front of the room, dressed casually in jeans and a soft, sage-green shirt, looking both nervous and excited. About twenty-seven of us gathered around him in an intimate semicircle.

Glancing around the room, I felt comforted as I recognized more than three-quarters of the group. We had been through a lot together and were already dear friends.

Jason stroked his beard, cleared his throat, and, without any further introduction, closed his eyes and started humming a wordless melody, called a *niggun*, in the Jewish tradition.

"*Lay De Dai Dai Dai, Lay Dai Dai Dai . . .*" Soon we all joined in. We picked up tambourines, rattles, and drums and created a holy concoction of sounds. Jason stomped his feet on the floor and together our voices soared, merged, harmonized, and slowly came down to silence.

We basked in the fading melody. I remembered hearing the same kind of joyous singing emanating from the synagogue around the corner from my apartment in New York. When I walked past, I was always slightly embarrassed by the enthusiasm and fervor of the congregants. Sitting here now, though, a door in my heart creaked open, and a whisper of holiness drifted in.

At that time, the Jewish renewal movement was just getting started; it would stimulate more interest in the teachings of Kabbalah and revitalize Jewish liturgy. Synagogues had begun to offer Jewish meditation and chanting services and classes in nondual Judaism. Many Jewish seekers had been leaving Judaism, drawn to Eastern religions such as Buddhism and Hinduism for their accessible spiritual practices. So many Jews left in search of spiritual answers that they were affectionately nicknamed *Ju-Bus* and *Hind-jus*. Those who returned to Judaism brought the meditation techniques they had acquired on Eastern spiritual paths back into the fold of Judaism. Although Jewish by birth, Jason, too, had studied Zen Buddhism, yoga, Advaita Vedanta, and modern psychology before becoming interested in Jewish mysticism.

Healing as a Path of Relationship

We looked at Jason expectantly as he paged through his five-inch-thick loose-leaf notebook, filled with the class curriculum. Based on the thickness of that notebook, no one was surprised when the one-year training became a two-year training, then a three- and finally a four-year training!

Jason leaned forward and said, "We need community in order to heal. We have all been wounded in relationship and we heal in relationship. Let me tell you how this training came about.

"I had written thousands of pages of notes, and after years of struggling with the Kabbalistic material, one day a door opened, and I received an implied hands-on-healing method that, to my knowledge, no one had yet discovered or employed. I saw how the Kabbalah is a path to healing as well as nondual awakening. By healing, I mean being in relationship to wholeness. Kabbalah is a living tradition, not a finished textbook. It encourages us to tread the same pathways of revelation and self-illumination that the great sages of the past did and to find our own way to our direct relationship with God."

I had some knowledge of Kabbalah from the little reading that I had done. I knew that in traditional Jewish circles, to receive the teachings of Kabbalah, the student was supposed to be male, over forty years old, and steeped in the practice of Judaism and the study of Torah, Talmud, and Halachah (Five Books of Moses, Commentaries, and Laws).

I didn't meet any of those requirements nor did my fellow classmates, except for those who were over forty and male. Our group came from all different religious backgrounds, and our common purpose was an interest in healing and spirituality. Within our group, we had acupuncturists, chiropractors, doctors, nurses, teachers, and housewives. Clearly this was not going to be a traditional Kabbalah class.

One Good Question

Jason continued: "I want to start with your questions. What are the questions that brought you here today? What are you wrestling with in your life, in your healing practice? One good question can be better than half a dozen answers."

I could barely contain the question burning like a hot coal in my soul, and I blurted out: "Does a person's shadow get bigger as they embody more light?" In asking the question, I reflected back on my experience with Sananda. How could he project so much light into the world and still have such a big shadow and unhealed personality? What's the use of all his spiritual teachings if he abused his power?

Jason looked at me with raised eyebrows as he contemplated his response.

"The Kabbalah has a lot to teach us about the union of opposites, how the light and the dark, good and evil, all arise from the same source—God. God is both dual and nondual and beyond any naming. By definition, God includes all of the opposites, all names and all forms. We will go into to those teachings deeply as we study the Tree of Life," Jason answered.

Perhaps through the teachings of Kabbalah I would also learn how to redirect the wild forces within me that yearned for union and kept searching for it in all the wrong places. I had heard that much erotic imagery filled the ancient Jewish texts, where the longing for God is compared to the longing for a lover from whom we have been exiled and to whom we long to return.

My own longings were still fueled by lust and my overheated second chakra. I longed to find a man with whom I could soar in Tantric union, a life partner who would be both spiritual and sexual, my version of the perfect fantasy man.

Preparing to Receive

To prepare our motley group to receive the teachings of Kabbalah, we did various exercises that challenged us to become more present to reality.

Jason introduced one of the first practices we learned, which he called *form anxiety*, with great passion. "We have a fundamental resistance to being in form, to being in a body. Yet it is the very material of our human lives that awakens us to God consciousness. We want to be able to meet God right here, just the way we are, with what we consider to be both our good and bad parts. Even our egos are holy and are a part of this wholeness."

Jason continued, "The ancient Jewish mystical tradition teaches us that we are already designed to receive God. We just need to make ourselves available to that which is already present within us. Before we can become one with everything, we also have to be present to our hidden unconscious aspects. That means we don't split reality into the parts we like and the parts we don't like. We have to include it all; otherwise, we won't be able to heal others. We will only want to fix them, because we can't tolerate their suffering or our own. So for this practice, we will just be with what is, without changing anything."

Practitioners of Zen meditation and Vipassana meditation will find this practice familiar; yet as Jason taught it, it had a slightly different flavor, because there was no one particular thing to focus on—everything in our experience was to be included.

As I listened to Jason's instructions, it seemed easy:

"Just sit. Don't regulate your thoughts or breathing. Keep your eyes softly open, so you don't get lost in dreamland. Simply be with whatever arises in this present moment. Don't save yourself from your anxiety, your restlessness, or your desire to be anywhere else but here. Simply be with what is. We will sit for ten minutes."

I adjusted my posture so that I felt more comfortable in the hard hotel chair. I sat there. No spiritual states, no lights, no euphoria.

Just me—being with myself—as I contemplated the endlessly fascinating geometric patterns on the carpet. I could visually travel along those carpet lines for only so long before I got bored. There was nowhere to go. No way to escape myself. I wanted to run, to move, to go outside—anything but sit there.

Just then Jason, as if reading my mind, said: "Notice when you want to move or leave the present situation. Don't stop yourself from moving if you need to, but simply notice it without judgment."

I fidgeted with my posture, crossed my legs, and changed my hand position. God, ten minutes is a long time, I thought. I can't wait for this to be over. I fantasized about lunch and imagined my menu choices. And then something that felt like nothing, happened. I didn't judge myself or my thoughts, I simply relaxed into nondoing and pure being. I experienced a state of just existing, without an agenda, simply resting in my own awareness, my own aliveness. I felt both separate and part of everything and everyone in the room. Perhaps this awareness lasted a second or two. Then Jason rang a bell and the ten minutes were up.

"How was this for you?" he asked the group.

I shared first, filled with a sense of excitement. "This practice could change my basic orientation to life. I can see how I am always running away and distracting myself to avoid simply abiding with my own discomfort, anxiety, and depression. I feel that I can just accept these parts of myself, rather than always trying to escape."

Jason responded, "Yes, in this practice we stop looking for someone on the outside to blame or to save us from the difficulties we experience in life. We just let them be without trying to change anything."

Over time, this practice created a new spaciousness within me. When my clients sensed this growing spaciousness, it created space for their disowned difficult feelings and sensations that never had been allowed to exist. Every difficult thought, emotion, or sensation that is allowed to exist is invited into the field of our attention and, therefore, into the arms of our own self-acceptance. Only then can it be metabolized and healed.

This radically shifted my way of working. I didn't need to have superhuman powers or X-ray vision to be an effective healer. Paradoxically, I could perceive more because everything that needed to be known appeared in this state of openness and presence. There wasn't any magic to it, but it was magical. In Hebrew there is a name of God called *Yechidah*, the intimate one. Being with my clients in this way became a portal to *Yechidah*.

A Powerful Exercise

Although I could navigate subtle states of consciousness with ease, I had much to learn about the intimacy of the relational field that is constellated between two or more individuals. This next exercise highlighted the way we project our reactions onto other people.

"I need two volunteers," Jason said. Hands shot up, and Jason picked a man and a woman and invited them to sit opposite each other in the center of the room.

He said to them: "I am going to give each of you a secret mission. I would like you each to embody a particular emotion, without showing it on your face or with your body language. Find some way to embody your mission with your energy. As you do this, be aware of each other and your inner reactions to each other. Those of you in the audience, I want you to tune in to your own inner reactions as you observe them."

He approached the volunteers and whispered their missions in their ears.

"So you can start your missions now."

The room was silent as we watched them. Gradually, I sensed a conversation in the form of energy fields between the man and the woman. It seemed as if the woman emanated something that radiated out of her heart in soft waves. These waves reached outward toward the man.

The man's energy felt more contained and powerful. I felt both repelled and attracted to this combination. If I had to say what his energy brought up in me, it would be the feeling of attraction and love. When I felt her energy, it also felt like love but less powerful, and I felt less drawn to her.

"Okay," Jason said to the two of them, "intensify your mission for just the last two minutes and then rest."

Once they had relaxed, Jason turned to the group. "What did you observe or feel in your bodies?"

One person said: "I thought she tried to send him love, and he rejected her by creating a wall in his energy field."

Another person said: "She seemed powerful, and so did he; it felt like their energies were in a battle with each other."

Jason turned to the two volunteers and asked: "What did you both feel? Tell me about your inner experience without revealing your mission just yet."

The woman answered first. "Well, as hard as I tried to do my mission, I didn't feel I was received, so I just tried harder."

Then the man spoke. "As I did my mission, I felt really good at first, invulnerable and in control. Then as we continued, I felt lonely, and I started to get very sad. It became harder and harder to hold on to the state I was projecting. I felt as I did when I was a little boy and nobody noticed me."

"Isn't it amazing how much gets constellated in this silent dialogue," Jason said. "Think of how much goes unnoticed in all of your relationships, in all of your interactions with people. Now, I am going to reveal their missions.

"To the man, I gave the mission to project the feeling of arrogance. To the woman, I gave the mission to project the feeling of love."

Jason turned to the pair and asked: "Did your experience feel familiar to you?"

They both nodded and shared how their feelings were similar to those present in their primary relationships.

"Each of you watching in the audience has had your own reaction to the feelings of love and arrogance. If love was smothering in your childhood, you may have experienced a negative reaction to the woman. If love was nourishing, you may have resonated with her. If you perceived his arrogance as a wall that blocked the receiving of love, this may be a familiar pattern from your childhood."

I raised my hand. "What if you were attracted to the arrogance and perceived it as love?"

"Well, which of your parents exhibited arrogance as a trait?" Jason countered.

"Well, my mother had narcissistic tendencies. . . . I guess there was arrogance in the way she always referred back to herself whenever I shared something with her. When I watched the male volunteer, I felt both attracted to and repelled by his energy. I realized that is exactly how I felt about my mother. I wanted contact with her and loved her, but I never felt that she really saw *me* or met *my* needs. It was always all about her. Yet I am always attracted to narcissistic men."

Jason introduced the concept of *riding the wave of transference*, to help us notice our transferential reactions to our clients so that we could be in clear relationship to them, not conditioned by our past. "That is the purpose of this exercise. To help us become conscious of energetic reactions and projections that are going on all the time based on our past relationships. When we can witness these projections, we can stop projecting them onto our partners, friends, and family. When we take responsibility for them, we become less reactive and more in touch with reality."

Through this lesson, I learned to hold my feelings of simultaneous attraction/repulsion to arrogant men as a viscerally alive feeling in my body. Only then could I be fully present for myself or anyone else. When I practiced this technique of holding my transferential feelings toward clients, it allowed for a tremendous amount of intimacy to occur, because my projections were not obscuring the present moment.

Over the next nine years, even though I witnessed this exercise three more times as an assistant teacher, I repeatedly perceived arrogance as love. That is how strongly the emotional patterning clouded my perceptions. Becoming aware of your projections and transference onto others is a lifelong practice. This one exercise sparked years of reflection on the way I felt attracted to men.

Now when I see an arrogant person walk into the room and feel that little spark of attraction/repulsion, I recognize it and name it. Then it is like a fog that clears, and I can simply see the person for who he or she is, without getting seduced or entranced by an image projected from my past.

Riding the wave of transference became an automatic practice when I sat with my clients. It became easy to stay connected to myself, attend to the interpersonal field between us, and use my new inner awareness to understand the client's relational patterns.

We attract the same patterns in relationship over and over again until we can recognize and heal the roots of our basic unmet needs. It takes courage to look within ourselves and transmute these wounds. When we heal, it's as if the hall of mirrors that keeps us searching for completion in "the other" disappears, and what is left is open awareness and clear relationship.

The Healing of Immanence

Jason shared, "Let me tell you how the idea for this healing came about. A woman came to my office to see me because of a problem with her quadriceps muscle. I had been working intently with the Shema in my personal practice, putting everything I experienced up against this great Unitive statement/prayer. The Shema says: 'Hear O Israel, the Lord our God, the Lord is One.'"

As I listened to Jason introduce this healing, I experienced one of those moments when my life seemed to come full circle. I was amazed that the same Shema that comforted me in my time of need as a thirteen-year-old in the synagogue was now being used for a healing.

Jason continued, "As I approached her leg to lay my hands on her and do a healing, I thought to myself: Where am I taking God from and where am I bringing it to? If God is One, then God is already present in this leg, in this physical problem, and in me. What if I simply receive this already present divinity? And so that is what I did, and as I came into relationship with the God immanent in her, I felt that same quality within me, and we simply rested there in this intimacy with God. When faced with God, she could not help but heal."

Jason then introduced us to the diagram of the Kabbalistic Tree of Life, composed of the ten *sefirot* arrayed with twenty-two pathways between them. The Tree of Life is considered to be the blueprint that God used to create the world and to create human beings. It is often talked about as a hierarchical ladder, with ten "rungs," stretching between heaven and earth. Each rung is an attribute or quality of God and is called a *sefirah*. When the Tree of Life is associated with the human body, it is depicted as if it is on the back of the body.

Jason pointed to *Malchut*, the last sefirah of the Tree of Life, and said, "Malchut means kingship and is associated with the physical world, the feet, and the Shekinah—the Divine feminine presence. Malchut is the furthest sefirah from *Keter*, which sits at the top of the Tree of Life and means crown. Keter is placed at the top of the head and is seen as the sefirah that is closest to God consciousness. Yet this healing challenges the notion that Malchut and the physical domain are separate or distant from God. We want to find the Divine right here, in this person, in this body, in this physical complaint, just the way it is.

"Let's practice the healing. Choose a partner, and choose which of you will be the healer first. To do this healing, you won't be running energy through hands or fixing anything. Sit with your client, put your hands on the side of their body, and set your intention to receive the already present divinity within them."

I chose a partner, a woman who talked about wanting to come to terms with the sexual abuse she had experienced as a child. Rather than focusing on her issue or

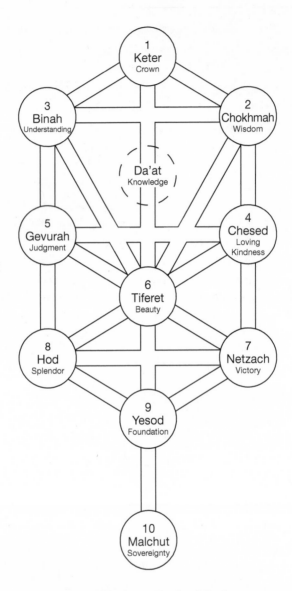

Tree of Life on Back of Body

trying to change her experience, analyze her, or heal her, I set my intent as instructed—to receive the already present divinity with in her.

As I did so, I felt a very subtle wavelike motion pass under my hands and through her body. The wave became the undulation of the life force itself, rising and cresting, descending and rising again. I didn't cause the movement, nor was I channeling energy into her body. I was focused on receiving the divinity within her. The movement subsided, and we rested in a shared space that felt like a holy communion. In that moment, we existed in a field of Divine embrace.

When we talked afterward, she said, "The healing seemed to allow the memory of my abuse to become unfrozen in time and take its place as part of the whole fabric of my being. I felt more intimately connected to my own wholeness when your hands were on me."

8

The Tree of Life

Princeton, New Jersey, 1994

Jason entered the room and walked to his chair. Though it was early in the morning, he looked at each of us with a penetrating stare. We felt the gravity of the moment as he choked up and said: "You are the first group to learn this work. I am hoping to receive one of these healings for myself one of these days!" he chuckled softly. "I will have to wait until you are all trained!

"We have been working with the Healing of Imma-nence, which is rooted in Malchut, this past year and a half. Ideally, that would be the only healing we would ever need. However, now we will begin our work with the other sefirot and learn of their unique qualities. To set our *kavannah*, our intention, and to prepare for our first encounter with the sefirot of *Gevurah* and *Chesed*, we will ritually wash our hands.

"I have placed a bowl of scented water in the front of the room, and one by one I would like you to approach the bowl and immerse your hands. We are not doing this for purification. You don't need to purify yourself in order to have contact with God or the sefirot. We connect to

God by starting from exactly where you find yourself right now, in this very moment. Simply set your intention to receive this tradition as you wash your hands."

We filed up one by one. As I approached the bowl, the scent of lavender oil and rose petals filled my nostrils. I closed my eyes and submerged my hands in the cool water. My inner sight opened, and I could see tiers of spiritual beings surrounding us, in acknowledgment of this rite of passage. In silence, I addressed these beings, praying to be worthy to receive the knowledge and wisdom of the Tree of Life. I returned to my seat with an open heart.

When the whole class finished, Jason started his lesson on Chesed and Gevurah.

"Chesed is found on the right side of the Tree of Life. We look at the Tree of Life as if it is on the back of a human being. Chesed is considered masculine and has the quality of unconditional giving and loving-kindness. It is associated with the right arm. It moves outward and flows. Gevurah is found on the left side of the Tree of Life and is considered feminine and has the quality of restraint. It is associated with the left arm. It contains and limits, like the womb, which contains the fetus as it grows.

"In all the pairs of complementary sefirot, you have the relationship between the masculine and feminine, like yin and yang in Taoism. One side cannot exist without its complementary half, and wholeness is the union of both sides. All of reality is formed by the relationship between these complementary pairs."

As I absorbed this information, I thought about the way all created things have a Chesedic and Gevuric aspect. For example, how an artist who paints uses the Chesedic quality of flowing colors; however, for the painting to be a painting, it has to be on a surface, a canvas, which has the Gevuric quality of restraint to contain the color and give the painting boundaries.

Jason continued, "The Tree of Life is not just a linear ladder from heaven to earth; it is a hologram of reality. The holographic principle means that within every part, you will find the whole. From the holographic perspective, no matter where you find yourself, God is present, embedded in each individual sefirah, or pair of sefirot, from the lowest to the highest."

Before he continued, Jason went up to the front of the room and drew a Tree of Life with a whole Tree of Life embedded in each sefirah of that Tree.

"What this means practically is that if you are working with a person in one part of the Tree, you affect the whole Tree and all the levels of consciousness. Through the sefirot and the multidimensional worlds of the Tree of Life, we can probe and understand the specific patterns of our individual journey on the physical, emotional, mental, and spiritual levels. The sefirot become a lens through which we understand all the unhealed aspects of our psyches, so that we can rectify them in ourselves and in our relationships. As healers, we can then also understand the larger patterns at play in the creation of disease or health."

As he spoke, I sensed these ever-expanding patterns of the Tree of Life present in my own body. I sensed how the primal combination of these forces forms every created thing and is powered by the indivisible unity we name God.

I contemplated the cells in my body, which automatically exchange fluids and nutrients with my blood. If there were no cell walls, there would be no absorption or

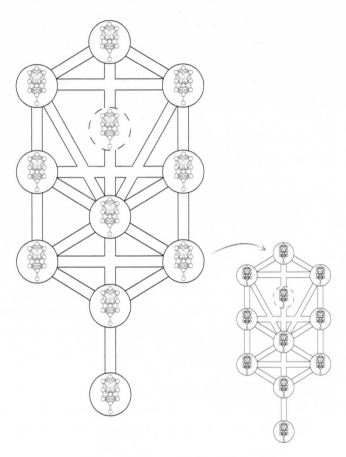

A Tree of Life within Each Sefirah

nourishment possible. Without veins and arteries, blood could not move to the different parts of the body. The cell walls and veins have a Gevuric quality and act as channels to move the nutrients through the blood. The blood has a flowing Chesedic quality, as it moves through the veins and arteries. They both complement and need each other for the proper functioning of the body.

Jason said, "When we learn the diagnostic process for these healings, we will look at different diseases in terms of their Chesedic and Gevuric qualities. The disease of cancer, for example, could be thought of as Chesedic or Gevuric, depending on the diagnosis. Leukemia, for example, [can be Chesedic because it] presents as an overgrowth of cells that spreads all over the body. In that case, it would need the quality of Gevuric restraint to balance the overgrowth. On the other hand, cancer can also be Gevuric, as in the case of an encapsulated tumor, because it is contained. Then it may need Chesed to create balance. You can see how understanding these qualities could affect the way you treat the disease. However, the diagnostic process is not this simplistic; it takes into account all levels of a person's reality, not just the physical."

Jason chuckled, "Since opposites attract, I am sure you can identify who in your primary relationship is more Chesedic or Gevuric? How do you complement each other or oppose each other?"

I immediately thought of Reuben, my now ex-husband. His need for order and structure presented as overly Gevuric in my opinion. Shoes lined up precisely by the door, clothes arranged by color in the closet, desk tidied with all the papers lined up precisely parallel to the edge of the desk! It used to drive me crazy.

He thought I was too messy. I thought he was obsessively neat. Compared to his high standards of order, I did appear to be disorganized. I liked the more Chesedic quality of my desk, with its organic arrangement. When it got too out of control, I cleaned it up and put everything into piles. Clearly the balance of Chesed and Gevurah changes in relationship to each person and their situation. These outer relationships with Chesed and Gevurah carried over to the emotional and spiritual levels, too. I displayed more enthusiasm, energy, and exuberance compared to Reuben. He had more containment and caution in his emotional expression. On the other hand, I often lacked the Gevuric quality of discernment.

Then Jason added something intriguing: "Each individual sefirah can have an *oneg* or *nega* relationship to its complementary partner. In Hebrew, oneg means "delight," and nega means "plague." The two words are spelled in Hebrew with the same letters in a different order: the letters ayin, nun, and gimel spell oneg; nun, gimel, and ayin spell nega.

"In Hebrew, each letter of the alphabet has a numerical value. So words with the same numerical value are said to have a mystical relationship with each other. Words with the same root letters also have a mystical relationship. So here with nega and oneg, which are spelled with the same letters and have the same numerical value, we are called to discover the deeper relationship between something that can be both a delight or a plague with just the turn of the wheel.

"For example, when someone comes in for a session and presents as being out of balance with Chesed, we look for the opposite aspect of nega Gevurah that underlies their presenting complaint, and vice versa. When we transmit the healing, we would start with a transmission of oneg Gevurah and combine it with oneg Chesed. In this way, the person gets to have a rectified transmission of the complementary pair of sefirot."

Then Jason said, "Here is a nega Chesedic statement: *When I give love to someone, I just want to give and give until I am exhausted.* Or, more prosaically, *Whenever I eat my favorite ice cream, I always overeat and devour the whole pint. Then I become sick.*

"We would look at the underlying Gevuric aspects to find the right proportion of restraint necessary to form a healthy relationship between these two sefirot."

As I reflected upon the oneg and nega aspects of Gevurah in my life, I realized that one person's straightjacket might be another person's version of a safe container. I reacted negatively when someone tried to discipline me, yet without enough boundary and structure, I became anxious.

I found this teaching about oneg and nega essential in understanding life's constant fluctuations. Every problem in life is based on our preference of one state over another state, and we constantly shift from nega to oneg and back again, depending on the situation and our relationship to it. In this new paradigm of healing, we traced the relationship between both sides of the complementary sefirot, bringing their oneg and nega aspects into more conscious relationship.

When nega and oneg cease to be opposites, a revelation happens; a new ability to be in relationship with both sides arises, a condition that did not previously exist.

I now understood the answer to my initial question about whether a person's shadow increased with their light. This teaching speaks to how the light always dances with the dark, the oneg with the nega, continually joined to each other in the dance of duality. The nondual consciousness includes both. When we don't split off the nega aspect from our consciousness, the nega aspects are en-lighten-ed. We can embrace both sides, without having to project our shadow onto another person.

Exploring the nega, however, didn't mean acting it out. I was about to experience this viscerally in the next exercise.

Cleaving to Sefirot

I felt excited as Jason announced, "We are going to learn how to cleave to a sefirah, one at a time, and then we will learn how to hold them together for the purpose of healing. Remember, the sefirot are not things, and they are not symbolic. They are Divine emanations that are dynamic and alive, constantly creating the world.

"So how does one cleave to a sefirah?" Jason asked. "Cleaving here is used in its lesser known meaning: to adhere to, to stick, to cling. In Kabbalah, cleaving is called *devekut*, and its usual meaning is communion with God. It also has a strong sexual connotation, as if you were cleaving to your lover.

"For our purposes, I would like you to cleave to the sefirah as if it were a brother or sister for whom you have a deep love. Doing it that way will take some of the sexual charge out of the experience.

"Let's try an experiment. Let's divide the room into two sides. The right side of the room will cleave to Chesed. The left side of the room will cleave to Gevurah. Are you ready?"

We answered "yes" and began to cleave to our assigned sefirah.

Immediately, I became conscious of a change in the room. The room polarized into two force fields, one spreading outward and the other more vertical, like a column or a wall. Where they touched, I perceived a shimmering boundary of light, forming a soft white haze as it permeated the room and enveloped us.

Jason said: "Now intensify your cleaving for just a minute."

As I increased the intensity, the white haze seemed to get thicker.

Relaxing afterward, one of my classmates joked, "Was that as good for you as it was for me?"

A Powerful Tension

Jason's attempt to damp down the potency of this exercise by using the brother/sister metaphor did not, in fact, succeed. We all buzzed with energy and aliveness each time we practiced the exercise.

One night after class, around ten of us had dinner in a private tatami room at a local Japanese restaurant in Princeton. Ravenous after the day's work, we ordered our food from a waitress dressed in a Japanese kimono. Within minutes, a stream of dirty jokes started flowing between us. We laughed until it hurt, oblivious to the other diners behind the shoji screens. The demure waitress covered her smile with her hand as she served our meal, but she couldn't hide her blushing cheeks. Apparently, we needed to discharge some of the intense energy generated by our early attempts to cleave to Gevurah and Chesed.

The next morning, we continued our exploration in dyads.

Jason said: "Choose a partner, sit opposite each other, and one of you cleave to Chesed and the other cleave to Gevurah."

I chose my friend Jim, an attractive married man with whom I had already had felt some sparks, to be my partner. I chose to cleave to Gevurah, and he chose Chesed.

We sat down on the patterned carpet under the fluorescent lights and closed our eyes to the suburban Princeton meeting room. We set the intention to cleave to our assigned sefirah. The room faded away as I felt a rush of upward energy.

Within seconds, my soul entwined with Jim's, as if we were wrapped around each other like strands of DNA, ascending through time and space toward a realm of light. I felt as if we were Adam and Eve returning to a paradise restored, and I could have stayed there forever, but in a few minutes Jason rang the bell, signaling that our exercise had ended.

It took several minutes to come out of this intense feeling of communion. Jim and I shyly looked at each other in awe, acutely conscious of the intimacy and strong energetic connection still present between us. I wondered if I had just met the partner I had been looking for.

"Did you feel that?" I asked. He nodded. There was no need for words.

Jim invited me to his room to talk after dinner. We shared how neither of us had come close to that kind of intimacy in our marriages. We came tantalizingly close to kissing, but we both pulled back, using Gevurah's power of restraint.

I had a restless night's sleep, fantasizing about a relationship with Jim. I began to understand the kind of boundaries and self-restraint I would need to be able to channel these forces for healing. No wonder the early Kabbalists stressed that one had to be married, supervised by a teacher, and grounded in the Torah and Halachah to work with the Kabbalistic teachings.

In our morning meditation, I couldn't settle my mind, which felt pulled in unwanted directions. Suddenly, I found myself lifted up to a different realm, filled with light and in the company of a Council of Elders. They pointed to a large book that apparently contained the Divine law.

An ethereal hand turned to a particular page, where I was shown the commandment to "not commit adultery," and I perceived that it had not been created as a moral law. Rather, like the rest of the Ten Commandments, they named already existing universal laws or principles. The commandment to not commit adultery described the best uses of our potent sexual energy, which could be used for procreation and life or selfish actions that caused harm.

Even though I was no longer married at that time, it became clear to me that an affair with Jim would be harmful to both of us, since he was married. The book of law was not about punishment; it outlined the actions that would be most beneficial as a foundation for our spiritual development.

I knew that I had free will. The Council of Elders held no judgment about what choice I would make; they simply showed the two paths of action before me and the results of choosing one over the other. Either way, learning would happen.

That evening, Jim and I walked arm in arm around the pond on the hotel grounds, then continued our dialogue late into the night in his room. Both of us struggled with the throes of longing and desire. We both knew an affair would be inappropriate and harmful. The energy still vibrated between us as we communicated from the deepest places of our hearts, intense longing and exquisite restraint equally present: a perfect, real-life example of the tension involved in holding any pair of sefirot together.

Sefer Yetzirah, an ancient Kabbalistic text, confirmed the experience we were having. In Aryeh Kaplan's commentary, he states:

But when the Sefirot [are arrayed opposite each other], a powerful tension is produced. When they are in such a mode, powerful spiritual forces can be directed and channeled. . . . the Sefirot had to be polarized to male and female sides generating tension and force. Just as human procreation involves male and female, so does Divine creation. . . . In making them correspond to the two hands, the Sefirot are polarized, creating spiritual tension. Once such tension exists, through meditation and concentration, the powers of the Sefirot can be focused and channeled.

The Third Thing

We came to call the product of this powerful and dynamic tension the "third thing," a force greater than the sum of its two sides.

The next day, we divided into dyads and one of us became the healer the other the client. Cleaving to both Chesed and Gevurah in our being, we allowed the presence of that union to come into our hands, and we transmitted that union to our client.

I focused first on Chesed and then Gevurah, then on both of them together. At first, they oscillated, then they unified, and that same electrical fusion, "the third thing," constellated as I put my hands on my client's body. I could only hold this electrifying union for a short length of time before I felt exhausted. My body was still an unprepared vessel to convey these healings.

9

Healing with the Sefirot

Princeton, New Jersey, 1995

My soul felt immediately at home with the language and concepts of Kabbalah. Jewish mysticism eventually became the portal through which I found my way back to a relationship with Judaism, a movement that would be deemed backward and inappropriate to traditional Kabbalists, who expected the student to be grounded in Judaism and its practices before studying Kabbalah.

We were given a reading list to supplement our experiential work in class. I delved into the texts with a passion that surprised me. I also read books about some of the great Kabbalistic mystics, like the Bal Shem Tov (Rabbi Israel Ben Eliezer) and the Ari (Rabbi Isaac Luria), and found to my astonishment that they functioned very much like the gurus I had been reading about in the yogic tradition. They gave meditation practices to their students and gave spiritual counsel. They monitored the daily details of their students' lives so that life itself became their spiritual practice. They, too, could transmit spiritual grace through a simple glance or a word. The main difference is that they were never worshipped as incarnations of God.

Sometimes while reading a Kabbalistic text, I would nod off into a strange dreamlike trance.

In class, I asked Jason, "Why is it that when I read these books on Kabbalah, I can't stay conscious for more than two paragraphs? I am not sleeping, and I am not awake. I am somewhere 'in the in between.' What's happening to me?"

"Ah . . . the technical term for that is . . . ," he paused for greater effect, "you have entered the Land of the Big Chickens!"

Everyone cracked up laughing.

Jason added: "These teachings are alive and are describing the energies of creation itself. To experience them is like going to the factory where energy is created. If you drift off into a trance state while reading a Kabbalistic text, it indicates that you can't yet stay present to the deep level of reality from which the teachings originate."

When I practiced the healings, I couldn't believe how tangible and potent they felt, to both me and my clients. They evoked in me a palpable, intelligent, and sacred presence, which could be transmitted through my hands.

Once, a woman came for her first healing with no prior knowledge of Kabbalah or Judaism. After the healing, she opened her eyes and said, "I saw and felt these golden circles of light over my body, and they were all connected. I felt imprinted with them."

Surprised, I pointed to a drawing of the Tree of Life hanging in my room, and she said, "Yes, that's what I saw when your hands were on my body."

As we completed our training, we learned healings with the seven lower sefirot: Malchut, Chesed, Gevurah, Netzach,

Hod, Yesod, and Tiferet. Aryeh Kaplan explains in his book *Inner Space: Introduction to Kabbalah, Meditation, and Prophecy* that an "awakening from below" has to happen before there is an "awakening from above." He notes, "Before any spiritual progress is attained, the initiate had to do the work of knowing their innermost self through unifying the lower seven sefirot."

We used the qualities of the sefirot as a way of knowing ourselves, our shortcomings, our projections, and conditioned thoughts, so that we could come into the present moment and sustain the awakened state. Each sefirah, pair, or triad of sefirot had its own unique application in the healing process. Only at the end of the training did we work with the more rarified sefirot of *Chokhmah* and *Binah*. The sefirah of Keter, in a similar way to the Thousand-Petaled Lotus at the crown of the chakra system, was considered too rarified to work with; it is the state of unity itself.

Rabbi Joseph Gikatilla, in his book *Gates of Light*, compares each sefirah to a room in a storehouse, in which each room is associated with a name of God:

Each room within the storehouse has a specific identity: one room has precious gems, one has silver, another has gold, while another has different kinds of food and another has drinks. If a person needs food, he may starve to death if he doesn't know how to get to the room. . . . So it is with . . . Names: there are Names in charge of prayer, mercy and forgiveness, while others are in charge of tears and sadness, injury and tribulations, sustenance and income, or heroism, loving-kindness and grace.

The inner work required to enter each of these rooms is akin to turning on a light in a dark room and becoming fully present to what is illuminated: ecstasy, disappointment, uncertainty, tenderness, anger, frustration, moments of intense connection and intense loss— basically all the aspects of being human.

I plumbed the depths of each of these "rooms" in the palace of my own life, and in this way, I forged my own direct relationship to the sefirot.

Since the sefirot are infinite, so is the healing process. Interacting with them is a spiraling down into the nature of the Self and reality, ultimately finding "God" in every part. Each Integrated Kabbalistic Healing (IKH) healing I received for myself revealed the intrinsic wholeness within my seemingly broken parts, unifying the oneg and nega aspects within me. Spiritually, it revealed the intrinsic wholeness present in life itself. In this manner, awakening and healing were intertwined.

By the end of three years, we had received a "palette" of different healings that could be employed to address the soul's journey through life.

The Tree of Life became the lens through which I viewed all my relationships. I gained more capacity to be in relationship with the totality of the person coming to me for healing, and it became easy to understand the formative patterns that may have led to their illness or current problem.

Becoming a Kabbalistic Healer

Initially, Jason encouraged all of us to use the techniques apart from our other work in order to master this very different healing paradigm, which made sense from a practical point of view.

By this time, I had a full healing practice in New York City, and I was already supporting myself as a BBSH healer; so when people came to me for a session, they expected a certain type of healing work. Learning these new techniques rooted in the Kabbalah created a conflict for me. If I chose to do an IKH healing, I had to explain this very esoteric work to my client. As a novice healer, I found it confusing to have two completely different modalities for healing.

I was eager to practice the Kabbalah healings, but I also didn't want to abandon the energy healing skills I had learned previously. I had a number of questions at that time: *Why and when would I be drawn to one modality over the other? Are there specific benefits to each type of healing? How can I track the results?*

From the beginning, I found that I used the different modalities at different times, depending on what the client presented. Certain situations seemed to call for repair of the subtle body with energy work before IKH healing could be most effective. Other times, I felt called to do a Kabbalistic healing first to address long-standing obstructive patterns.

Most of my friends seemed to do the same thing in their healing practices, even though Jason implied that his work operated at a deeper level.

Once I asked Jason, "What do you see happening in the energy field as we do the healings?"

"Well, let me tell you what I observe," he said. "It is so interesting. There is energy moving throughout the field in a way that looks chaotic on the surface; however, underneath, it looks like the whole energy system is being reorganized. These healings are not energy based. You are not giving someone energy when you do them; instead you are cleaving to God qualities and transmitting that union to the client. The healings are nonlocal and non-linear. You are affecting the deepest level of reality as you do them, as if you have moved the underlying foundation stones of a building, and then the whole building realigns as a result."

IKH work helped identify the forces underlying the illness or condition but so did the correct assessment of the chakras.

Both were useful, and it became part of my own learning process to choose the right modality for the client. I remember I had one early healing success with a man who was able to get off the list for a heart transplant after a series of healings. When I went back to look at my notes, I saw that I had employed both types of healing modalities during a series of eight or so sessions.

In my experience, the two systems do not function in the same manner; they feel fundamentally different in origin and flavor. The life force takes different paths in each system and creates different experiences along the way. However, since all esoteric maps attempt to describe the same journey from separation to Oneness, they do cover a lot of the same territory.

Both the Tree of Life and the chakra system demon-strate how blocked energy channels create disease, and both systems show how our inner wiring is designed to be a "receiver of God" and that our sense of separation is never real, just a function of our perception.

The Diagnostic Process

Along with the skill of embodying and cleaving to pairs of sefirot and transmitting their union through our hands, Jason presented a diagnostic process that became the basis for our approach to the Tree of Life as a tool for healing.

The diagnostic process wasn't a fixed technique; it required a beginner's mind each time I sat with a client. It was challenging because there was no one correct healing to choose, though some were more indicated than others. It required staying in a relational process with the client, cultivating an attitude of not knowing and a willingness to sit with uncertainty as the right healing organically revealed itself.

While sitting with clients in the diagnostic process, I would have intuitive leaps of understanding that enabled me to ask questions of the client that seemed psychic in their origin, such as: "Was your mother critical and judgmental? Did you give yourself away to authority as a child? Did you feel as if the atmosphere in your childhood home was poisonous?" But really these questions had their roots in the relational pathways of the Tree of Life.

A deep rapport of understanding manifested between myself and my clients, because of this empathic connection and because "brokenness" was not the focus of our exploration.

With the Tree of Life as the roadmap, the patterns of cause and effect, light and dark were revealed as part of the exquisite complexity of the soul's journey. Afterward, clients would give me feedback in the language of the sefirot without any prior knowledge of the healing, and almost miraculously their lives would change in the very area of the sefirot that I had chosen to hold. This was even evident in my growing long-distance healing practice.

By the time of our graduation, I was an assistant teacher for the second incoming class. On the day of graduation, we each were called into a private room to sit in front of Jason and receive his blessing. When my turn came, I entered the room and sat opposite a beaming Jason. He joyously conveyed words of praise that touched my heart. I knew that I had a future as a teacher with the school, so graduation was not an ending, just another beginning.

10

A Growing Dissatisfaction

Omega Institute, New York, 2002

By 2002, I had been a teacher at the IKH school for nine years. I taught introductory workshops on the East Coast, at Esalen in California, and in Germany. I also led super-vision groups and created graduate seminar presentations. I loved teaching, and I was being groomed to take over more responsibilities. For many years, I truly felt that I had found my calling.

I had moved to Princeton, New Jersey, a few years earlier to be physically closer to the school so that I could attend more staff meetings. By now, there were more of us on the teaching team, and together we devoted many hours to support Jason and help him develop future pro-gramming. The school became central to my life and healing practice. The blanket of security that the posi-tion provided allowed me to move yet again and buy my first house in the beautiful town of Lambertville, New Jersey, along the Delaware River.

Everything appeared to be going well, and my future at the school seemed assured. I had camped inside Jason's head for so many years that I could accurately predict how he would answer most of the students' questions. Yet more and more, I didn't know how to separate my own answers to those questions from his. I began to feel the need for individuation.

One day in early spring 2002, I sat listening to Jason's remarks at an introductory workshop at the Omega Institute in upstate New York: "Life is short, and then you die. In light of that sobering fact, what questions do you have?"

Although I, too, had opened workshops with these same words many times, this particular day they penetrated my consciousness as if I had never heard them before, bringing up questions that I had previously not allowed myself to entertain: *Is this where I am supposed to be? Do I want to keep teaching for the school or explore other areas of training? Is it perhaps time to move on?*

During the past few months, I hadn't felt as enthusiastic or idealistic about teaching as I had in the beginning years. Perhaps the cause was physical, I hypothesized, because I had been feeling so tired. Maybe I had Epstein Barr virus or chronic fatigue. For the first time in years, I felt an inner dissatisfaction creep in and a dragging weariness.

Over the next several months, this feeling of dissatisfaction continued to grow.

Jason had created a new spiritual practice and training, which he called Impersonal Movement, that I found challenging. For Jason, the practice was his leading edge, and he presented it with great passion.

The practice employed a form of moving meditation, holding pairs of opposites in one's consciousness in an embodied manner. It brought the practitioner very quickly into a glimpse of nondual awareness. Everyone else seemed to love the practice; however, I always felt irritated afterward, and the "circuits" in my brain felt like fried wires. I stayed with it, completing the training; however, my inner guidance knew that the practice didn't match the needs of my energy system—I just didn't know why.

When I reported my reluctance to do the practice, Jason treated my complaint as a resistance to nonduality. He said, "Not everyone is ready for this practice; it is very advanced."

My pride got engaged on that one, so I tried harder to please. The more I tried to do Impersonal Movement, the more my "resistance" to the practice grew. In hindsight, I now know that it was not the right practice to support the improvement of my Kundalini process. But I didn't know that then. And I didn't know what to do.

I tried to go along with the program, but eventually I felt like the one person who called out the emperor for having no clothes, while everyone else claimed to see his beautiful garments. I couldn't fake my lack of enthusiasm for the practice any longer.

From a practical standpoint, I couldn't imagine leaving the school; yet by this time, I wanted true spiritual guidance more than I wanted the comfort of my known world. I had reached a crisis point. I wasn't growing spiritually, and I wasn't receiving the help I needed.

I started to pray every night from the depths of my being for direction and guidance. "Please, God, show me the next step; show me what to do next!" I pleaded. "Please help me find a teacher who can help me."

Surprisingly, my prayers were answered a lot sooner than I had expected, and suddenly I found myself setting out on a new path.

Part III

Kundalini

The Vedic Path to Enlightenment

II

Answered Prayers

New York, March 2002

When the student is ready, the teacher will appear.

—unknown

The phone rang the night before a planned trip to upstate New York with my friend Susan.

"Dani, can we change our plans?" she asked. "I just heard that my friend Dr. Ken Porter is hosting a talk by a swami about Kundalini Science this weekend in New York City. I want to go—do you?" I received an immediate inner *yes*, and we rearranged our plans to register for the two-day seminar.

That night before going to bed, I looked up the definition of *Kundalini*. I found that the word has a Sanskrit root, meaning "coiled," and in the yogic tradition, Kundalini describes Shakti, the Divine feminine principle of awakening. This force of awakening is said to remain coiled at the base of the spine in the first chakra until "she" is released, usually by meditation.

Ultimately, she rises up to the top of the head to unite with Shiva, her masculine principle counterpart or pure consciousness. This union leads the meditator to experience self-realization. I went to sleep excited to learn more about this explanation of spiritual development.

In the early morning hours on the day of the workshop, I lingered dreamily between waking and sleeping. Suddenly, I had a fleeting but distinct impression of an orange-clad figure standing at the foot of my bed. He appeared in a flash and was gone just as fast, so I didn't think much of it until I walked into the seminar meeting room in a midtown Manhattan office building later that morning. Standing there at the head of the room in monastic orange robes was the very figure I had seen in my room.

He stood about a foot shorter than he had appeared in my vision, and a palpable spiritual force emanated from him, magnifying the impression of his stature. He had a shaved head and a close-cropped, grey beard. I noticed how he carefully assessed our small group of ten people with a stern expression and inquisitive, dark, deep-set brown eyes that glittered. His eyes grazed over me in an impersonal way, yet I had the uncanny impression that he knew just where I was struggling spiritually.

When I approached him to say hello, my heart pounded, and I could barely breathe. A deep, soul-to-soul recognition washed over me as I looked into his eyes, which twinkled despite the intense gravity that pulled my attention upright; they seemed to say, *Snap out of the dream! You asked for this. If self-realization is what you want, get serious!*

I had never met anyone like him, and I knew in a flash of clear insight that my prayers for help had been answered.

An American woman named Joan Shivarpita Harrigan stood next to him. Her short, silver hair framed her benevolent face like a soft helmet, and she wore light, tangerine-colored Indian clothes, the sign of a *brahmacharini,* a female renunciate. She introduced the swami with his full monastic name, Swami Chandrasekharanand Saraswati, and told us we could call him Swamiji for short and that we could call her Shivaji.

At the time I met Swamiji in 2002, he was seventy-two years old, in vigorous health, and had been training Shivaji in Kundalini Science for more than sixteen years. Together they had started a consulting service called Patanjali Kundalini Yoga Care (PKYC). Even though Swamiji lived most of the time in Rishikesh, India, he came to America once a year for an extended visit. For the rest of the year, he held phone and Skype consultations with Shivaji on all their "cases"—the people who came to them for spiritual guidance.

Shivaji started the presentation with a brief story of how she had met Swamiji in India. "I first met Swamiji during a spiritual turning point when I realized I needed to leave my teacher and the ashram where I'd been living and working for the past ten years in order to progress spiritually. I was disillusioned and desperate for effective guidance."

Exactly how I am feeling right now, I thought to myself.

She continued, "In a rather miraculous series of events, I met Swamiji, and he gave me a spiritual practice which, in a very short time, removed the block that had been limiting my spiritual progress." Shivaji's eyes teared up as she spoke. "When I went to my room to do my practice, I had a sublime inner experience. All of a sudden, my consciousness went up into the light, and I had a vision of Swamiji's Great Master, an immortal being of light.

"Shortly afterward, Swamiji rushed in and exclaimed, 'The Great Master himself has initiated you!' Swamiji later recognized me as the person he had been waiting to train in his lineage of Kundalini Science for all these years, due to our past-life karmic connection more than three hundred years ago. We both have memories of that life in which I was like a mother to him after the tragic death of my daughter to whom he had been betrothed since childhood.

"Since that time, Swamiji has trained me to help people discern how to progress in their spiritual life through knowledge of Kundalini Science, lifestyle instruction, and direct experience obtained through individually prescribed yogic practices."

Swamiji took over the conversation when Shivaji finished, launching into the day's topic, Kundalini Science. He began by dispelling some false or misleading notions that people held.

"Kundalini is not just energy; she is Shakti, the Divine force within," he said with great emphasis. "She is the Divine Mother; she is omnipotent. She is radiation, vibration, and light." He paused to let his pronouncements sink in, then continued, "She is the first subtle power of pure consciousness to manifest into reality."

I was stunned by the clarity and enthusiasm with which he spoke. He went on, "She sometimes has a bad rep here in the West!"

We laughed at his use of slang. His heavily accented English required Shivaji's translation every few sentences, so he spoke slowly and with great emphasis. As I listened, I was able to perceive a huge aura around him that seemed to condense downward when he talked.

Shivaji further clarified one of the most common misunderstandings about Kundalini. She said, "In the West, people have taken to using the word *kundalini*, with a small 'k,' to define weird movements of energy in the body. Those movements of energy are actually called *kriyas* in Sanskrit and are caused by movement in the *vayus*, which are the five major subtle functions of *prana*. One of those five major vayus is called Prana vayu, and we use a capital 'P' to distinguish it from the general way the term prana is used as a generic term for energy in the West."

Swamiji jumped in again. He seemed to be illuminated from within as he spoke, now in a soft voice: "Kundalini Shakti, with a capital 'K,' is not energy. She is supreme grace and love, imperial majesty, intelligence, the life of the life force, self-illuminating, forgiving, the source of all emanation, the principle of sound, pure joy, and bliss. To understand how Kundalini works is to understand the inner workings of all spiritual traditions. She is the force behind all awakenings and has been called many different names in different traditions, including Holy Spirit, Divine Mother, Shekinah, Holy Grail, and Shakti, to name a few.

"Some think she is dangerous because they've heard about people who've had difficult experiences. But she is not dangerous. She wants you to be enlightened and wants to bring you to the Source."

He went on to explain: "In her unreleased state, Kundalini remains coiled at the base of the spine. Under ideal circumstances, when Kundalini awakens, she has access to different *nadis*, or energy channels, which vitalize both the subtle body and the physical body. *Sushumna nadi*, a central channel that she uses, travels along the spine.

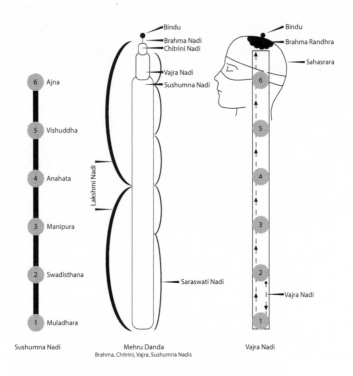

Nadis Used by Kundalini Shakti

Adapted from *Kundalini Vidya* by Bri. Joan Shivarpita Harrigan, PhD.

"In the West, yoga teachers often talk about Sushumna nadi as if it were the only channel through which Kundalini can rise. According to our tradition, there are six different channels through which Kundalini can rise: Lakshmi nadi, Saraswati nadi, Vajra nadi, Sushumna nadi, Chitrini nadi, and Brahma nadi. Three of these—Vajra, Chitrini, and Brahma nadis—are nested within Sushumna nadi. Together, they form the *Mehru Danda*, which is the proper description of the central channel. Two nadis, Lakshmi nadi and Saraswati nadi, are outside the Mehru Danda.

"At PKYC, our services help people cultivate the right inner conditions for her to do her work. She will not stop until she finishes the job and arrives at *Bindu*, the top of the head. But she needs the right support to carry out her mission."

Shivaji told us a little more about Swamiji's past. "Swamiji met his own master, Bodhanand Maharaj Saraswati—a lineage holder of Kundalini Vidya, or Kundalini knowledge which was founded in the fifteenth century by Gomatagiri Maharaj—when he was twenty-seven years old. Swamiji awakened through a very rare and intense Kundalini process that took over eight years to complete.

"During some of that time, he couldn't function, and someone had to take care of him. This process enabled him to understand the many different ways Kundalini works in the subtle body and enabled him to become a teacher. At the time of his own realization, he wanted to leave his body and not come back, but he was told by his master that it wasn't time yet and that he had work to do before leaving would be possible.

"Swamiji was a *sanyasi* and wandered the length and breadth of India twice as a beggar. He learned Ayurvedic medicine from his master and for many years treated the mothers and babies he encountered as a service to the Divine Mother. His masters gave him the task of guiding qualified students to improve their spiritual lives and prepare them for self-realization. He gained his expertise and knowledge from his lineage and from thirty years of intense spiritual practice and study.

"During his wandering days, he was initiated inwardly by three great Indian adepts: Tirumular, Agastya, and Kakabhusanda. He also learned much from other wandering yogis and from direct observation of the people he counseled spiritually. When his master Bodhanand Maharaj was about to die, he told Swamiji that he had been chosen to take over as the heir to the lineage of Kundalini Vidya."

Over the next two days of the seminar, Swamiji and Shivaji presented the theoretical overview of their approach, sharing information not previously offered in the West. They described in great technical detail the nature of the six different risings, illuminating both the gifts and the problems that are associated with each. They spoke about the many ways Kundalini can become stuck, diverted, or blocked in any one of the chakras or nadis, unable to complete her journey up to Bindu at the top of the head.

Shivaji said, "Most people who are afraid of Kundalini have read the accounts of individuals who suffered for years because of a stuck rising without effective spiritual guidance."

As they talked, I contemplated the parallels between the different nadis used in Kundalini risings and the different pathways connecting the seven lower sefirot in the Tree of Life. Whether one calls her Shakti or Shekinah, this force is the way the Divine opens us from "below" to the experience of union and self-realization.

Swamiji went on to explain: "Most people on the spiritual path already have a Kundalini rising that has gotten stuck due to poor lifestyle, toxins, or wrong practices. We see people who have done more than thirty years of meditation, and their Kundalini still has not risen to Makara point in upper Ajna chakra. Makara point gives the seeker the ability to catch the gap between thoughts and have 'no mind' experiences.

When Kundalini reaches Makara point, we consider that to be the *beginning* of spiritual progress!"

Shivaji added: "Many people who come to us have reached a point where they are longing for liberation and are ready to commit to spiritual life. They reach Makara fairly quickly, within a few days or by the end of their first retreat. The initial release of Kundalini can happen spontaneously when the energy system is vitalized and the mind is concentrated due to correct spiritual practice.

"Sometimes, however, it happens through especially intense experiences such as trauma, sex, childbirth, and esoteric methods. It can also rise due to the blessings of a realized being or saint. In our consultations, we discern the state of your subtle body, your physical body, and your mental and emotional concerns, and we give you gentle spiritual practices to do on an individual basis."

Vajra Rising

Swamiji and Shivaji went into more detail regarding the different types of Kundalini risings on the afternoon of the second day. They described each of the six different nadis through which Kundalini could rise and the kinds of experiences that a seeker would have with each type of rising. My ears perked up as Swamiji started to describe the *Vajra rising*. Swamiji declared loudly and with great emphasis, "Vajra rising is the *sex* rising!"

He chuckled a little bit, knowing that hearing those words from a celibate monk would amuse us. Then he looked straight at me.

I wanted to disappear through the floor.

Shivaji took over and said, "The Vajra rising is a deflected rising. This means Kundalini doesn't enter Makara point and can't proceed to Bindu at the top of the crown to achieve spiritual completion. All people have a Vajra nadi. This nadi is used energetically by everyone to produce the Unitive experience during orgasm. But in Vajra rising people, the nadi is further powered by Kundalini. Kundalini supercharges both ends of the nadi—at the second chakra and the brain centers in Sahasrara. This is why it can create special abilities and also sexual addiction.

"Sometimes, Vajra rising is called the *left path rising*. This is based on a misunderstanding people in the West have about Tantra, which is misrepresented as a method to merge spiritual and sexual practices."

Swamiji turned toward a diagram posted on a board and pointed out the route to Vajra nadi, saying, "Vajra nadi begins at the genitals (Swadhistana chakra), goes down toward the base of the spine to Muladhara chakra, and then travels straight up to the crown, or Sahasrara, without opening and purifying the chakras as it rises. Then when Kundalini descends, the person loses the glimpse of Oneness they received and, thus deprived, can become depressed.

"A Vajra rising doesn't enter Makara point at the top of Sushumna nadi. When the rising has been corrected, Kundalini can then enter Makara point in upper Ajna chakra. Reaching Makara point heralds the *beginning* of stable spiritual progress."

Shivaji said, "A Vajra rising can give a person great gifts—the gift of healing, great intelligence, special talents, intuitive insight—but it doesn't stabilize those gifts or their process. It gives a person a laserlike capacity to mentally focus and charge their desires, intentions, and emotions with prana. Through this intense outward focus, the person can make his or her desires and intentions dynamically effective in the energy field of another person. This talent is the basis for 'charming' techniques, magic spells, and the ability to transmit effective energy healing; it's real magic."

Oh, dear! I groaned inwardly as I immediately recognized the attributes of a Vajra rising in my own experience. In fact, I realized I could be a poster child for this rising. It explained the ease with which I learned energy healing techniques and my interest in channeling.

When a new man entered my life, I would become obsessed, my whole psyche overwhelmed with fantasies of seduction. My Vajra antennae were so finely tuned, I'd bet I could pick out all the Vajra rising men in a room within ten minutes. I'd recognize them by their sexual vibes, giving away how they were always on the prowl for a conquest. Half the men I had slept with probably had a Vajra rising going on!

As I listened, I realized I had most of the other characteristics described for a Vajra rising: hormonal imbalances—yes; sexual addiction—yes; neurotransmitter deficits—yes (And a big *aha* on that one! No wonder I couldn't do Jason's Impersonal Movement practice. I already had brain burnout, and doing the practice just irritated my condition.); healing abilities—yes; occult and astral skills—yes.

Shivaji remarked, "These special abilities are a special temptation. People with this rising and with these gifts say, 'Yes, but I am doing good in the world with my gifts.' However, there is a price to pay, because the use of these special abilities depletes the mind and the prana system. Using these special abilities is inadvisable if you want to support Kundalini Shakti's mission to improve your spiritual life."

Ouch!! That would just about eliminate my whole livelihood!

The description of a Vajra rising pretty much explained my encounter with the dark guide Sananda—who most likely, in my humble opinion, also had a Vajra rising.

After the presentation, we were invited to approach Swamiji to say goodbye. He smiled at me but then said in a stern voice, "So which type of Kundalini rising do you think you have?"

I answered wryly, "The *sex* rising," placing the same emphasis he had given the word. He laughed and with great kindness said, "It is not hard to fix. Come to our retreat for two weeks, and we will help you."

A New Path Begins

The first step in scheduling a two-week retreat with PKYC was an assessment of your Kundalini process based on a detailed written report that covered your spiritual, mental, emotional, and physical history, as well as family of origin, traumas, and life difficulties.

That night, I went home and immediately started writing my report. In twelve pages, I revealed my promiscuous escapades with men, as well as my out-of-body experiences, healing capacities, esoteric studies, and physical problems.

I felt too ashamed and mortified to write in my report the fact that during the past few months I had been having strange astral encounters during the night with gargoyle-like beings wanting to have sex with me. Or that I'd actually awakened during one of these encounters, screaming and pushing one of these horrific beings away. Instead, I concluded: "I really want to have a sexual and spiritual partnership with a man."

Swamiji must have been quite amused by that one, a typical Vajra rising statement.

I sent in my written report, along with the requested copy of my palms and a full-length photograph of my clothed body. A few weeks later, I had my first phone assessment with Swamiji and Shivaji.

They spoke alternately, with Swamiji starting: "You've come into this life with a Vajra rising, with a block at the throat chakra. This rising is common in the Jewish esoteric tradition. You have always had a strong interest in the occult, and you have good intelligence, open brain centers, and an interest in the arts. Your spiritual development is very good, but you have had the wrong guidance, and you have very poor discernment. To correct the Vajra rising process will be easy with the grace of Kundalini Shakti herself."

Then I asked, "Can you tell me what happened in the dream experience I wrote about in my report? I have asked a lot of people about it but have never had a satisfactory explanation." I reminded them that one night, I awoke from a dream paralyzed and afraid because I couldn't move. I felt electricity running up and down my spine, and there was this loud buzzing noise. Afterward, I fell back asleep, and I went into a lower realm and zapped people with the light coming from my hands.

Shivaji responded, "People often report a kind of sleep paralysis, which is a normal part of REM, or rapid eye movement, phase of sleep. The electricity going up and down your spine could indicate the movement of Kundalini in Vajra nadi. In Vajra nadi, Kundalini can stimulate the brain centers, giving the person access to the subtle astral levels. It gives easy access to other realms.

This access is intermittent, as Kundalini then descends. Vajra nadi is not a stable process."

"Oh," I said, "I have wondered about this for years. Your explanation is so clear. I was so afraid that night; now I am relieved to know I wasn't in any danger."

Swamiji then abruptly interrupted and changed the subject. He started talking about the Jews in Cochin, India, who lived in peace amongst the Indian people for many years. He seemed to infer that I had a past life in Cochin. Then he spoke of two Jewish sects from the time of Christ, the Dead Sea sect and the Essenes, and alluded that the Essenes were the more spiritual of the two and that the Dead Sea sect had become corrupt. Although I don't remember his exact words, what he said penetrated my soul, touching long-buried past-life memories. As he spoke, I felt as if I had lived in those times.

He said, "In the time of Jesus, the Jewish priesthood had become corrupt. In their corruption, the priests cultivated deflected Vajra risings among the initiates to open their brain centers in order to produce extraordinary intelligence and esoteric gifts. Then the corrupt priests would use the initiate's knowledge and skill. It served the priests' political agendas to *not* divert the rising into Sushumna, the central channel, so self-realization would not be achieved; therefore, the head priests remained in an authoritarian position of power. Gradually, the esoteric knowledge of how to divert the rising for self-realization was lost, keeping the paradigm of enlightenment or liberation available to only a few."

Once again, I felt queasy hearing this information, again sensing it was knowledge somehow buried in my own past.

I booked the soonest available spot for my first two-week retreat in Knoxville, Tennessee, with excitement and some apprehension. My dear friends Susan and Martha joined me, and I knew that we would be able to support one another if the going got rough.

I didn't realize until much later that I had entered a completely different paradigm of awakening from the one taught by Jason Shulman. This new paradigm returned my focus to the subtle body and the chakras, a framework I was familiar with from my study at the Barbara Brennan School. However, this was a much deeper and more precise level.

The Kundalini model that PKYC presented challenged the way in which the word "awakening" is so vaguely used in the West for the whole spiritual journey. They differentiated between different stages on the spiritual path, defined by the progress of Kundalini's arousal and elevation: no Kundalini rising, the initial release of Kundalini, partial rising, deflected rising, intermediate rising, faux full rising, full rising, Upper process, complete process, expanding process, and culminated process.

It is because of this precise knowledge that they could specifically pinpoint the correct spiritual practices to support and improve a person's spiritual life to best suit their individual needs. For this reason, in contrast to popular Kundalini yoga classes, they never gave out group practices.

In August 2002, I drove down to Knoxville from New Jersey for my first retreat, feeling as if I were on a flying carpet. I sang out loud to the country music on the radio, sensing that I would soon be entering a master's domain and a very different reality.

12

Kundalini Initiation

Knoxville, Tennessee, August 13–23, 2002

Shakti makes the impossible possible.

— Swami Chandrasekharanand Saraswati

When I arrived at Shivaji's house in Knoxville, I saw two brown feet and a bit of an orange robe peeking out from under the slightly raised garage door. I definitely had the right house! Her modest suburban ranch house sat on a quiet street that had lush green lawns and old magnolia trees. I parked the car and wheeled my luggage down toward the basement door, passing carefully tended flower beds studded with small statues of saints.

Entering the basement apartment that would serve as our retreat house for the next two weeks, I found myself in a white-carpeted living room. A palpable hush greeted me, along with a unique aroma of incense mingled with the pungent smell of Indian spices and Ayurvedic medicines. The focal point of the room was a beautiful altar filled with pictures of saints from all the spiritual traditions. A painting of Kundalini Shakti, the Divine Goddess, draped with a garland of orange flowers, occupied the center of the wall above the altar. Framed pictures of the other masters in Swamiji's lineage encircled her.

The remaining expanse of the living room was divided into three yoga stations, each supplied with a square, foam meditation platform topped by an orange meditation cushion, a chair, a timer, and an orange towel. Tall screens separated each area for privacy. I guessed we would each claim a station to do our practice. I felt a tingle of excitement as I anticipated receiving my own custom-tailored spiritual practice.

I explored a bit further and found three bedrooms, a bathroom, and a storeroom for Ayurvedic medicine. The bedroom next to the storeroom had a little handwritten sign on the door with my name on it, so I wheeled my luggage inside and sat down on the bed. The whole space had an ambiance of quiet sacredness.

Martha and Susan arrived a few hours later, and we caught up over a light supper of soup and veggies that had been left for us on the stove. At around seven p.m., we heard the door open upstairs, and Swamiji and Shivaji came down, singing a soft Ommmmm to alert us of their presence. They welcomed us and told us that we would be called up individually to receive our practices the next day.

Shivaji explained: "You are here for yourself. Stay internal and quiet, no gossiping or loud laughter." (She had to remind us more than once of that rule!) "Once you receive your practices, you will be doing them four times a day for the duration of your stay. It will take us a day or so to get up and running, so be patient."

The next morning, we were called upstairs one by one to meet with Shivaji and Swamiji to receive our practices. Martha and Susan went upstairs first, so for most of the morning I browsed through the selection of spiritual books. I found an entire shelf devoted to Kabbalah and picked out a few books to read later.

Finally, it was my turn, and I went upstairs and entered a pleasant, sunny sitting room. Swamiji sat in a chintz-covered armchair; Shivaji was nearby. He looked piercingly at me and said: "You have holes in your aura, and your whole subtle body is weak."

I understood in that moment why I had been so exhausted lately. Prana had been leaking from my energy system like water leaking from a hole in a bucket. I wondered to myself if the holes allowed those scary gargoyle creatures to attack me at night. Gross!

He added: "And you have subtle body toxins due to poor lifestyle choices, and your prana vitality is low. Tomorrow you will receive Ayurvedic medicine and oils that will help repair your energy system to support your Kundalini process."

Swamji turned to Shivaji and said: "You show her the practices."

Shivaji sat down on the floor with me and demonstrated the sequence of the ten postures and *pranayamas* (breathing practices) that were to be included in my practice. I copied her while she watched, and afterward she made minor adjustments to my gestures or posture. Having practiced vigorous yoga for years, I was surprised at the simplicity and ease of the practices.

Shivaji explained, "The postures work with the five vayus—which are the flow of prana, or energy, associated with each chakra—that sustain your life. Your practice is designed to make the vayus move and combine in particular ways so as to improve your Kundalini process. We recommend that you don't do your regular Hatha yoga practice with the set of practices we give you; otherwise the energy is sent in too many different directions."

I groaned inwardly. I had just completed a year-long yoga training and found great pleasure in attending two or three yoga classes per week. After this retreat, I would be doing all my yoga at home. She gave me a timer, as each posture had to be done for a prescribed number of minutes, and I went downstairs to join my friends.

The First Day

By eight a.m. the next morning, the three of us lined up like little ducks in a row at our yoga stations, ready to start our practices. The door upstairs opened, and Swamiji and Shivaji came down and sat in front of us. We could see them, but we couldn't see one another due to the screens between us.

I said a silent prayer asking for help and blessings, then began doing my postures. I immediately perceived a pair of disembodied eyes surveying my subtle body as I started the practice. Whose eyes, I didn't know.

Energy moved between the right and left sides of my body. At one point, I stood with my hands clasped and pointed upward, and light descended over me from above like a cosmic shower. I opened my eyes and noticed Swamiji looking directly at me, as if he, too, noticed the descent of light. He quickly closed his eyes. A feeling of pride washed through me, as if I had caused that light to descend myself with my prowess as a yogi.

Later that morning, I wandered into the storeroom to browse through the many Ayurvedic herbs on the shelves. I gasped as I came face to face with Swamiji. I hadn't even heard him come downstairs.

He looked me right in the eyes and shouted: "Pride! Your main issue is pride."

I turned beet red and didn't even attempt to defend myself. I mournfully realized the truth of his accusation. I had come to the retreat puffed up with pride about my status as a senior teacher at ASOS and secretly wanted acknowledgment for my mystical capacities. What is embarrassing now is how little I actually knew at the time and how far I still had to go on the spiritual path.

Swamiji's fiery "silver hammer" came down upon my head as he shouted: "You are lost! You have lost your way!"

His words pierced my heart like a laser beam. I started to sob, realizing his words were indeed true.

Swamiji never missed a chance to pulverize the crud of my egoic tendencies and attachments. He pounced on my pride like a cat stalking a mouse. He showed no interest in coddling my personality or fostering any sense of specialness. As painful as this moment was, it also felt like a relief.

I slid down the wall to the floor. "Swamiji, please help me. I don't want to keep making the same mistakes lifetime after lifetime."

These words, neither logical nor premeditated, poured out from the depths of my soul. And Swamiji never let me forget them! In that moment, time stood still, and I sensed Swamiji "seeing" through me, seeing the bag of traumas I had carried for lifetimes.

He said, "You have had a tragic fall from grace in a past life. You were exiled from your Jewish tribe and allowed to die. That's the past. Kundalini will heal you. You need to forgive and forget."

Now my tears flowed uncontrollably. This theme of exile from the Jewish tribe had always been present as a holographic theme of my soul, yet I had never been able to explain it in a logical fashion to myself. Now Swamiji just named it, pulling it out into the open from the hidden recesses of my past. He named something I knew but didn't know, and it produced a heart-wrenching grief. My soul felt as if it had shattered to pieces.

I immediately flashed back to a similar heart-wrenching grief that came up when I had read a passage in the book *Initiation*, by Elisabeth Haich, in which she described a past life as an initiate in the Egyptian temple of the Pharaoh. Haich related passing her final initiation in the temple, only to break her vows of celibacy by allowing herself to be kissed by a man.

In one moment of fiery sexual passion, she lost her connection to her elevated consciousness and lost her powers. She died a tragic death, mauled by the very same lions that she used to be able to control with the power of her mind. Her soul was exiled from her spiritual tribe; gradually she climbed her way back to her former status as a high initiate by reincarnating lifetime after lifetime with this same man, who became her husband in her current lifetime.

When I read this passage so many years ago, I could barely breathe, and I exploded with emotion and pain, just as I did in this moment, standing bare before Swamiji. Her story must have echoed my own deep-seated themes of exile, sexual shame, and loss.

As my spiritual quest deepened, these same exact themes came up to be healed in my current life. The theme of celibacy still challenges me, and while I don't believe it is in any way a requirement of the spiritual path, it has been part of my journey.

Swamiji, noticing my stricken face, said in a soft voice: "Don't dwell in the past. The Divine Mother forgives. Focus on the present and do your practice."

He turned and walked quietly upstairs. The inner work had begun.

13

Reaching Makara Point

Knoxville, Tennessee, August 2002

In the morning before my eight a.m. practice, I did self-massage using specially prescribed Ayurvedic oils, covering my whole body and head. The oils removed toxins that built up due to the intensity of our practices. Then I joined my two friends in the living room, and we chanted opening prayers together before starting our individual yoga practices. I found great comfort in hearing them breathing next to me as they did their practices behind the screens.

My practice took over an hour and fifteen minutes to complete, and the postures were not as easy as I had originally thought. I strained to hold some of them for up to five minutes. Relief came at the end when I sat in meditation, reciting the mantra selected for me by Swamiji.

Swamiji wanted us to keep notes of our experiences in practice. While in most Zen, Buddhist, or nondual circles, reporting one's experiences in meditation is given little attention, Swamiji used the notes of our experiences to adjust our practices and to help us understand how Kundalini Shakti worked in our own subtle and physical bodies.

He never told us anything in advance. He said, "You tell, then I say." He enjoyed this process of seeing how each person's journey manifested different challenges, and he took his job very seriously. I think we were like science projects to him.

Each person was given individual attention through several one-on-one consults during the retreat. I came to appreciate the rarity of having a spiritual master track and update my spiritual practices on a regular basis. In addition, we were given Ayurvedic herbs to support our physical and subtle bodies. Through my many consults with Swamiji over the years, I realized his knowledge of the subtle body far surpassed anything that could be found in books.

By the end of the first evening, I crashed. Too exhausted to do the last practice, I sat on my cushion for just a few minutes of meditation before collapsing into bed.

That night I had the following dream:

I haven't cleaned my house in a long time. There is dust everywhere. When I look down at the floor, there are two big, eel-like snakes poking their heads out from under the furniture in different parts of the room. I am scared that if I clean the room, they will come out.

Snakes are a well-known metaphor for Kundalini, who, when coiled in her unrisen state, can look like a sleeping serpent. Indeed my subconscious knew that change was coming in the "house" of my soul.

I thought everything went well the next day. I didn't experience anything out of the ordinary in my morning practice, other than my mind running on and on with worries about the past and the future. My whole body shook rapidly as the thoughts seemed to convert into energy and disperse.

Swamiji apparently thought otherwise. After lunch, he summoned me upstairs and said: "You are blocked below Ajna chakra, between the eyebrows, right below Makara point. There is a neighborhood spa that does *shirodhara*. I want you to call and get an appointment as soon as possible."

"What's shirodhara?" I asked.

"It's an Ayurvedic treatment in which a steady stream of herbalized heated oil is poured on Ajna chakra between the eyebrows. It will help with your toxic buildup. I will be with you in spirit during the treatment."

I called the spa and booked an appointment that afternoon. I had my own car and meticulously wrote down the directions, which were quite simple. I hadn't realized the effect of being secluded on retreat until I ventured out into the world.

As I drove, I became quite disoriented and made numerous wrong turns. A ten-minute trip took twenty minutes, and I arrived late. I had the feeling that Swamiji knew I had been driving in circles. Despite my late arrival, the spa owner greeted me graciously and ushered me into a treatment room. I lay faceup on a table, and she positioned a heated container of oil over my Ajna chakra. Soon warm oil dripped in a steady stream from a small spout onto my forehead and slid down the back of my head into a container that held the overflow.

I drifted into a deeply relaxed state of Divine bliss, losing all sense of time and place. When the hour ended, I showered and washed my hair three times until all the oil rinsed out. I drove back to the house without missing a turn and arrived just in time for the late afternoon practice.

During the fifth pose of my practice, seated cross-legged, hands clasped in front of my chest, my head fell backward, and I couldn't move. I felt energy rise upward along my spine, and on my mind screen I saw a green light with a dark purple center. Suddenly my consciousness pushed through the dark purple center and burst into the light. My whole body started vibrating, and I had very little sense of self. I dropped into a deep meditation and couldn't complete the rest of my practice. I had to lie down, and I remained enveloped in sublime bliss for the rest of the night. Without a doubt, I knew that something profound had just happened.

The next day, Swamiji and Shivaji read my practice notes and confirmed that the Vajra rising had been diverted into the central channel, Sushumna nadi, and had ascended and pierced the diamond hard cap, called *Itara Linga*, that protects the gateway to Upper Ajna chakra.

I felt exultation! I had reached Makara point! I now knew that my spiritual path was finally on the right track. I can't convey in words how sacred this experience felt. It all happened so quickly that I didn't have any remembrance or any felt sense of the diversion into Sushumna nadi. I do know that the shirodhara treatment cleared the way for the process to rise, and that without that intervention, the process could have remained stuck for a much longer time. I felt gratitude, amazement, and awe that these practices produced such real and tangible results.

I could see how it might be easy to mistake this sublime experience for the endpoint of the journey.

Renovation and Restoration

The renovation and restoration process kicked in immediately after I reached Makara point. I experienced lots of burping, pain, spontaneous rapid breathing, and convulsive movements in my body every time I did my practice.

In her book *Kundalini Vidya*, Shivaji likens this process to being in a purification plant, with smelly toxic stuff flowing outward to be released. Makara gives one the ability to witness the river of waste going by from the safety of an observation tower, so that one doesn't get polluted or destabilized by the waste.

Shivaji explained, "After reaching Makara, Kundalini Shakti systematically clears the chakras in the subtle body, working from her elevated position in the subtle brain. This type of clearing is a permanent, spiritually driven upgrade of the entire energy system. As the chakras are purified, all of your hidden wounds are brought to the surface so that they can be healed. This unloading process requires stamina and guidance, for at times you can be overwhelmed by the intensity of your feelings, which can range from consuming bliss and the sense that you are beyond ordinary life to a feeling of utter despair and worthlessness.

"The great gift of the unloading process means that the seeds and roots of your karmas are eventually completely burned so that they no longer influence you. This can only happen after Makara point. Therapy and healings cannot uproot and burn the seeds. Only Kundalini Shakti can, after reaching Makara. Since we all have lifetimes of karma in our bag of *Chitta*, or the part of the mind that is the storehouse of *samskaras* [latent impressions] and *vasanas* [desires], this can take some time. Your daily practice helps support Kundalini's work in clearing the subtle body."

I could actually feel the drive of Kundalini Shakti working relentlessly within me to repair my subtle body. At the time, I had no idea that my own renovation and restoration process would take more than twelve years to complete.

One morning during meditation, I heard an internal voice that said: "Self-judgment and self-hatred are what keep the cycles of pain repeating in your second and third chakras. Forgive yourself, and love yourself." Then later I heard: "God gives us all these riches and we don't see them."

I had been experiencing a great deal of shame and remorse as my lower chakras purged. Shifting my awareness to "God's riches" felt like a relief. It opened the door to gratitude again, and I had enormous gratitude for the opportunity to be on retreat with Swamiji.

However, after four more full days of practice, I felt blocked and overwhelmed by my own negative thoughts. My body felt like a sack of old baggage, too heavy to carry any farther. I dragged myself to my cushion and prayed inwardly for help as I started my practice. Strange sensations swirled through my belly as energy gathered and thrust upward. I gasped and didn't know what to do.

At that very moment, Swamiji, who sat meditating in front of me, opened his eyes and said, "Lie down!"

As soon as I landed horizontally on the floor, my body automatically went into the yogic "fish" pose, with my head, neck, and spine arched back and my arms bent at the elbows supporting my body. I screeched as a huge dark writhing mass of energy released upward from the base of my spine through the top of my head. I surrendered to the movements as my body convulsed a number of times, and finally the purge finished. I curled up into a ball and rested under my blanket. The Sanskrit mantra *Om Namah Shivayah*, which means "I salute the Self within you," spontaneously arose in my consciousness.

The next few days passed quickly, and, more and more, I felt filled with light.

An Outing

By the end of the first week, on Sunday, Shivaji came downstairs and announced: "Just do your morning practice; today we will have an outing!"

In the late morning, the three of us bundled into the back seat of Shivaji's old station wagon, with Swamiji in the passenger seat and Shivaji at the wheel, and off we went to the Great Smoky Mountains for a sublime picnic.

As we rolled into the parking lot, the car had barely come to a halt before Swamiji leapt out and brusquely walked to the edge of the forest. Whenever Swamiji went to any sacred site, he communed with the (bodiless) adepts of the area who watched over the place and who would then teach him their special spiritual methods. Swamiji loved learning the methods of all the different spiritual traditions.

He raised his arms upward in prayer and then bent them back over his head, crossed his arms and stretched them upward, then brought them down in prayer in front of his heart. Shivaji quickly followed, performing her own salute to the adepts. The trees appeared to whisper back in response. I gradually came to understand that Swamiji was no ordinary swami. He was a member of a group of adepts who met monthly on the full moon, in their celestial bodies, to discuss the problems of the world and give spiritual aid where appropriate, for the betterment of all humanity.

When Swamiji and Shivaji returned to our group, they guided us to a lovely trail, where we found a secluded spot perfect for our afternoon meal. I was seated on a blanket, surrounded and shielded by grand old trees, and our sylvan scene reminded me of being in an ancient forest hermitage at the feet of a great sage. Swamiji unpacked the stacked stainless-steel containers of food that he had lovingly prepared for us that morning. One by one, he filled our plates with fried popadam, samosas, dal, rice, and cooked vegetables. I savored each morsel as we ate in silence. After lunch, we had a peaceful conversation, then went to the banks of a creek and meditated for a short period.

On the drive home, Swamiji sat silently in the car in an elevated state, barely connected to his body, apparently still communing with the mountain adepts. Shivaji glanced at him and said: "Son, are you okay?" (She sometimes called him "son" based on his past life with her, when she was his foster mother.)

After a pause, her words registered, and he answered: "Junk food, Mom."

Shivaji understood and cheerfully explained, "We're stopping for fried onion rings and root beers; fast food brings him back down to earth."

So after our sublime picnic, we stopped at a fast-food place and joined Swamiji for some onion rings and soda!

We arrived home in time for our late-afternoon practice. The energy in the room went wild, as the mountain energies permeated the room and our practice. My breath came rapidly, and my whole body shook as these forces amplified my practice. When the shaking subsided, I had to lie down to rest.

It felt like the mountain adepts provided extra energy so that Kundalini Shakti could scour my subtle body and discharge the biggest chunks of old karma she could find!

Last Days of Retreat

Kundalini Shakti continued the relentless renovation and restoration process, concentrating on my heart chakra. The pain of past heartbreak and betrayal weighed heavily in my chest.

On our last retreat day, I sat at the kitchen counter and watched Swamiji as he prepared our lunch. Swamiji qualified as a bona fide "foodie" in the Indian tradition, and he delighted in showing us how to prepare nourishing Ayurvedic cuisine. When he cooked, he focused intently, channeling all his love and devotion into the food until it became permeated with Divine vibrations. As soon as I ate his devotionally prepared meals, the Shakti in the food seemed to cross the blood-brain barrier and suffuse my brain with light.

Sitting there watching him, I couldn't believe I would have to reenter my normal life in just a few days. I felt so different, as if illuminated from within.

Swamiji handed me some mangoes to peel. I tried to maneuver the paring knife under the skin; however, the mango slipped out of my hands and shot across the counter. My hands seemed disconnected from my mind at that moment. I felt so otherworldly and expanded that objects had no meaning or substance to me.

Swamiji said: "Give that back to me; go sit down."

Swamiji didn't seem to have a problem cooking while being in an exalted state. I, however, felt woozy and wobbled over to the dining table to sit down.

I glanced down at the table, surprised to see a beautiful strand of small white pearls resting upon each of our plates.

Swamiji said, "This gift is for your initiation at Makara. We call you three 'the three graces.' You have all worked hard these past two weeks."

My heart broke open, and I sobbed at this kind gesture. So much love and acceptance emanated from him that I cried louder and louder. Lifetimes of unworthiness and shame came up to the surface and dissolved in my heart in the warm waters of my tears.

Eventually Swamiji said: "You are being too emotional! Stop crying; you are hurting your subtle body."

In that moment, the tears subsided, and I could feel the beginning of self-forgiveness creeping into my heart.

During lunch, I asked Swamiji, "How long will this renovation and restoration process take?" Typical of most Westerners, I, of course, wanted immediate results.

He answered: "Who can say? Kundalini Shakti tries her best. She will not quit until the job is finished. It depends on how you support her. You need right rest, right nourishment, deep intensity in your practice, and strong yearning for the Divine. You have a weakened energy system because of the deflected Vajra rising. I can't tell you how long it will take to repair it. Do your practice!"

14

Repair and Restoration

New Jersey, 2002

I left the sanctuary of the retreat feeling translucent and ethereal, as if the oncoming cars could pass right through me. But I came down to earth when I discovered that my car needed a major repair before I could hit the road. The synchronicity of the situation didn't escape me as I wondered if this might be a parallel to the repair process now raging through the vehicle of my subtle body.

After waiting three hours for the car to be fixed, I finally headed north on the highway toward New Jersey. Like a person coming out of a dark cave into bright sunlight, I tried to adjust my vision, but everything felt too fast and superficial. The events of the past two weeks replayed in my mind and seemed even more surreal the further north I went.

Did I really reach Makara? How would my life change? I imagined that everyone I met would recognize this new light blossoming inside me. I didn't imagine that this fundamental change in my being would in fact take years to metabolize.

I stopped that night at a roadside motel and had a very restless night's sleep. At four a.m., I awoke with an endlessly repeating question in my mind: *"Who is it that is making such changes in the upmost body with such tenderness?"*

Apparently, my subconscious had noticed the momentous changes created by the movement of Kundalini Shakti. I arrived home after two days of driving and hibernated. I tried to adhere to the retreat schedule. I cooked my own food and did my practice twice a day. That dwindled down to once a day after the first month.

I walked around feeling "out of sorts," unanchored, lonely, and depressed. I didn't fit in anywhere. I couldn't bear going out to my favorite bars and cafés in the neighborhood because the density of the energy repelled me. It was hard to discern the difference between my perimenopausal hormonal moodiness and Kundalini's inner fireworks, which continued to absorb all of my attention.

For each person, this process will be different, depending on the condition of their subtle body, physical body, and life situation. It would be boring to recap all the many inner experiences I had during those early years. I was dedicated to doing my practice and kept daily practice notes. Over time, I noticed a steady and gradual improvement in my physical vitality.

Often, while lying in bed, I experienced intense involuntary pumping movements originating from my pelvis. They resembled the movements of coitus in reverse, as if my body were trying to eject all the male energy that had been pumped into it during past sexual encounters with men. My second chakra was healing itself. I couldn't imagine making love to a man now, while the past was being relentlessly purged from my body night after night.

When I consulted Swamiji about these kriyas (involuntary movements), he said, "Kundalini Shakti makes shaking medicine because of lack of vitality in your subtle body. Do your practice regularly, and it goes away." With this explanation, I began to trust my body's gyrations and spasmodic movements.

After two years, the intense pelvic shaking abated and my mind filled with light at the end of my practice. Light poured through me like a molten river descending through my crown, and afterward a profound stillness arose; there was no sense of personal self, just an all-pervading feeling of presence. I often reported that I had "no mind," just silence and light.

Swamiji commented, "When the mind receives light, it erases the problems until they are freed from the subtle body."

Swamiji also suggested I look up Yoga Sutra I.36: *Vishoka va jyotishmati*, which means: by perception of the luminous state within, which is free from sorrow, steadiness of mind is established.

Knowing this was a strong motivation to keep doing my practice.

Pre-Makara, I would *try* to meditate; now meditation happened automatically with no effort. These periods of "no mind" lasted a few minutes at most, but I had a glimpse, a taste, of the Vastness beyond the chattering monkey mind. It gave me a baseline to come back to again and again.

I simultaneously experienced elevated consciousness and base-level chakra repair. This is because my brain centers had been opened through the Vajra rising, which gave me access to other spiritual planes. However, just because those doors were open, it didn't mean that I had full residency! My consciousness still wavered; it was far from one-pointed, and my lower chakras were still undergoing repair. My job was to simply support this inner process with right rest, food, and practice.

Upper Process

Once enough of the initial repair work is completed in the subtle body, Kundalini enters *Upper process,* the next phase of Kundalini elevation. There is still some repair going on, but Kundalini Shakti has enough clearance to start moving upward, toward Bindu at the top of the head, where she will eventually complete her journey.

In my third year of post-Makara Kundalini process, I was surprised when Swamiji said, "Your Upper process is changing to a Tree of Life process."

This was the first time I had ever heard him say that the Tree of Life patterned how energy moved in my subtle body! From then on, Swamiji used the language of the sefirot to describe my Upper process after Makara.

I kept trying to have him relate it to the other Upper process routes described in *Kundalini Vidya,* but he kept repeating that I couldn't compare the two systems, that they worked differently in the subtle body.

For the first time, I really understood that we are all wired differently for the "God" experience.

Although Unitive consciousness is singular, the paths to it expressed by the different spiritual traditions produce different spiritual experiences along the way. Each tradition has its methods to prepare the initiate for the opening to the Divine within, here called Kundalini.

One of the ways the Jewish spiritual path opens up is through an "awakening from below." The seven lower sefirot are rectified and balanced through meditation and contemplation to create a subtle body that can receive the "Divine influx," which comes in the form of light.

In Tree of Life language, Upper process is centered in the parietal lobes (Chokhmah and Binah) and Keter (the crown, comparable to Bindu).

Swamiji explained in a phone consultation, "After your process shifted upward through the lower chakras and finally reached the heart, Tiferet was activated; and because Tiferet is in the central column, it connected with Keter at the crown, and this allowed *Da'at* to open."

This was a revelation for me. Da'at is the mysterious eleventh sefirah; it is a non-sefira in the Tree of Life. It is not officially part of the ten sefirot that make up the Tree of Life, and, for this reason, it is always drawn with a dotted line and has no pathways leading toward or away from it.

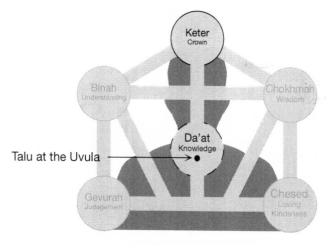

Da'at

Da'at means "knowledge" in Hebrew. It is not intellectual knowledge; it is the kind of knowledge that is so deep that you become it. At Da'at, the knower, the knowledge, and knowing become one. One could say that Da'at appears everywhere in the Tree when there has been a real revelation through direct experience.

Swamiji said, "Da'at is related to an opening in the subtle body called the Talu, at the uvula [near the tonsils], which opens to the basal ganglia at the base of the brain. Its opening allows for real knowledge to be accessed from the universal Source. When this happens, the central column, the light pillar, opens and gives real spiritual knowledge, not intellectual learning. When these three are stimulated and Da'at becomes activated, the release of endorphins further opens up this triangle and produces the feeling of bliss."

For several months during this period of my practice, my body had been spontaneously going into *kechari mudra*, a yogic position in which the head is thrust backward and the tongue presses into the soft palate. This spontaneous kriya apparently stimulated the uvula at the back of my throat. Here again, my "inner wiring" combined the two paths of Kundalini and Kabbalah.

Swamiji loved brain science. He studied the brain and made many comments as to what happened in the different lobes of the brain as Kundalini repaired the subtle body after Makara.

He often said, "Kundalini Science is brain science! Kundalini's command post after Makara is the brain." Then quoting the title of Daniel Amen's book, he'd say with great gusto, "Change your brain, change your life!"

In *Kundalini Vidya*, there is a map of the entire chakra system superimposed upon the brain.

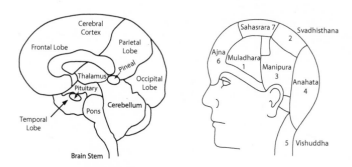

Chakras and the Map of the Brain

Adapted from *Kundalini Vidya* by Bri. Joan Shivarpita Harrigan, PhD.

This level of correlation between the chakra system, Kundalini, and the Tree of Life fascinated me, and my own body became the laboratory of my exploration. I became really curious about the differences and similarities between the chakra system and the Tree of Life.

I came across a book called *The Mystical Heritage of the Children of Abraham*, written by Daniel Feldman, a disciple of a Western adept named Dan Bloxsom. I was astonished to find a Tree of Life diagram that described similar characteristics to a deflected rising!

The illustration shows the movement of consciousness in the Tree of Life, upward to the crown in a zigzag fashion, called the "Lightning Flash." A wall of fire blocks the gate between Power (Gevurah) and Wisdom (Chokhmah). There is another wall that prevents further movement up the Tree between Understanding (Binah) and the Crown (Keter). This path is called the "Way of the Wizard." It similar to that of a Vajra rising in the sense that the wizard seeks to influence physical reality with special powers and/or to acquire power/knowledge out of a selfish desire for personal benefit.

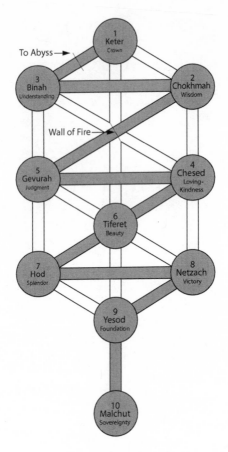

Way of the Wizard

Adapted from *The Mystical Heritage of the Children of Abraham* by Daniel Feldman.

For this reason, an initiate ascending the Tree in this way would either be blocked by the "wall of fire" or be redirected into the Abyss before reaching Keter and Unitive consciousness. Similarly, before a Vajra rising is corrected, the initiate is deflected from reaching Bindu at the top of the head.

I immediately sent copies of the book to Swamiji and Shivaji. The main difference between this image and the description of a Vajra rising is that Vajra rising happens within the central column, and here the movement starts on the right of the central column. The diagram validates the statement Swamiji had made earlier, that Vajra rising process is a technique of the Jewish adepts who cultivated brain-center openings for knowledge, which equals power, but they either withheld or forgot the esoteric technique to divert Kundalini into Sushumna nadi. In this text, I also found other alternative Tree of Life diagrams, which could possibly correlate to the other types of Kundalini risings described in *Kundalini Vidya*.

It was hard for me to discern how the chakra system and the Tree of Life worked simultaneously in my Kundalini process, because at the time I would just have the subjective experience in my subtle body, and I didn't understand what caused it or where I was in my process.

Most Kabbalistic texts focus on the downward flow of light, which leads to the creation of the world. I wanted to understand how the ascending process worked to prepare our physical body and subtle body for the union with the Divine.

My hypothesis is that through the balancing of the complementary pairs of sefirot, a person becomes unified on four levels, described in Kabbalistic language as the four worlds: *Assiyah*, the physical world of activity and making; *Yetzirah*, the unconscious, emotional, astral level; *Briah*, the archetypal level; and *Atzilut*, the level of nearness, of God realization.

When these levels are coherent, we are ready for the "Divine influx." When there is enough balance in the seven lower sefirot of the Tree of Life, and very deep yearning for God, by grace the gate of Makara opens. It is plausible that Da'at in the Tree of Life is akin to Makara point, even though Da'at appears at the throat, not in the upper brow. Perhaps that is why Da'at is called *secret knowledge*.

Stepping into the Abyss

Gradually, my "normal" life became normal again, and I continued to work as a healer in private practice and as a teacher and supervision group leader for A Society of Souls.

However, I faced a growing internal dilemma with Jason's new Impersonal Movement practice. I didn't want to do it, and I couldn't find a comfortable way to withdraw from the Impersonal Movement retreats. My whole identity as a senior teacher in the school would be in jeopardy if I didn't attend the retreats. If I didn't keep up with his new practices, I would be isolated from the group.

Yet to do them would be to betray myself and the growing inner sense that Swamiji was now my spiritual teacher. But leaving the community would be like committing professional suicide. Just the thought of it made me feel sick with fear and panic, as if I were jumping off a cliff.

I had a scheduled phone meeting with Jason to plan my role as a teacher in the next three-year training. Paradoxically, rather than face quitting, I thought I would try for a raise.

The phone rang at the appointed time, and after some initial chitchat, I said, "Jason, I would like a salary increase for these next three years to match what I would be making in my private practice for those days. I haven't had a raise in six years."

There was silence.

Finally he said, "Well, the school can't afford the raise you're requesting. My expenses have gone up, and there are less students registered in the classes."

"I don't know if I want to continue," I said, trying to stall for time and prevent the inevitable. "Let me think about it," I said, and we ended the call.

I think we both knew the issue wasn't really money. I had already been withdrawing energetically, and he had noticed. I already had a foot out the door.

After I hung up the phone, I stared blankly out the window of my new house. How am I going to pay the mortgage? I wondered. My panic and anxiety escalated as I envisioned myself homeless and without work. Catastrophic thinking, buried deep in my Jewish genes, surged to the surface like a dormant virus.

I hung in there for about six more months. I couldn't make a decision.

On a beautiful spring day in May, I drove to Jason's house to attend my monthly supervision group, a group that had been together for almost ten years. The group members were my dearest friends and fellow teachers, but I knew the time had come to either commit or quit.

I swallowed hard and addressed Jason and the group. "I need to end my commitment to this group and my teaching commitment to the school. I have learned so much and love you all, but I feel the need to move on. I will miss this monthly support and comradeship, and most of all I will miss working with the students. I love seeing their growth and progress through the training."

After what felt like a long, silent pause, Jason, looking down at the floor, said, "Well, I wish you well and give you my blessing. It is a big loss, but the school will certainly continue without you."

His last sentence surprised me. It felt so cold; nevertheless, I breathed a sigh of relief as a huge weight lifted off my shoulders.

Much to my surprise, several other teachers withdrew from teaching. Within the next two years, our whole teachers' group dispersed. Apparently, we had all gone as far as we could go, and the need for individuation and change became evident within each of us.

Although I stopped teaching for the school, I still led a few supervision groups, which allowed me to bridge this huge change of circumstances. Like a trapeze artist suspended in mid-air between swinging rungs, my old life was left behind and even as I reached out for the next rung, I couldn't figure out how to structure my new life.

15

Homecoming

Princeton, New Jersey, 2003

Whatever is truly seen will in time become true. A true perception is an energetic act that activates the energy of connection . . . it activates your potential because it's been seen.

—David LaChapelle

I found myself isolated and lonely without the ASOS community and our regular gatherings. The PKYC consultees didn't gather as a group to support one another's Kundalini process. We were each to live as an "ashram of one person" by maintaining a *sattvic* (peaceful) lifestyle at home: good rest, good food, and minimal distraction to allow Kundalini Shakti to do her job. Despite my regular consultations with Swamiji and Shivaji to evaluate my progress, I felt a bit unanchored.

Thirsty for contact with like-minded others, I jumped at the chance to attend a Krishna Das *kirtan* (chanting the Divine name) in a barn behind someone's home in Princeton.

As the founder of the kirtan movement sweeping the world, Krishna Das already occupied a revered place in the community of new age seekers. A nice Jewish boy from New York, his whole life changed when he met his Indian guru, Neem Karoli Baba, who encouraged him to chant in Sanskrit. He was a former rock star wannabe, and his deep baritone voice, loaded with testosterone and devotion, inspired many seekers to start chanting in Sanskrit. I looked forward to the evening.

When I arrived at the concert venue, the streets around the house overflowed with cars. The classic, white-clapboard, black-shuttered farmhouse sat back from the road on sixty-three acres of land. We were directed to the barn, which had seen better days and probably would have qualified for demolition. People sat on chairs, pillows, or on tiers of hay bales.

Undeterred by the rain that began leaking through the ventilation slit at the peak of the roof, Krishna Das began his opening chant, filling the barn with an invocation to Hanuman, the Monkey God, in the Hindu devotional hymn, the Hanuman Chaleesa. I closed my eyes and basked in the flow of mantras as the longing in my heart for God/Spirit/Truth/Presence exploded, and the barn seemed to turn into a holy temple.

Afterward, we were invited inside the house for coffee and tea. I sought out the owner, curious about the type of person who would invite more than three hundred strangers into her home. I wandered through the beautifully furnished rooms until someone pointed her out, an unassuming woman standing near the kitchen entrance.

"I am so touched that you hosted this event at your home," I said as I introduced myself.

She introduced herself as Patricia and continued, "Yes, this is part of a vision that I had to start a center, called Center Heart, dedicated to living life with the understanding that *There is but One*. I am hoping that Center Heart will be devoted to nondual teachings and meditation. We are already holding meditations here twice a week. It would be great if you could join us."

I came the following week and immediately felt at home in the group, a motley assortment of fellow seekers who came together to sit in silence for an hour. After the meditation, we each gave voice to our inner experience from the depths of silence and tried to keep the superficial story level at bay—with varying success. The weekly meditation became a nurturing container as I continued my solo practice at home, and Patricia became a dear friend.

One evening, Patricia announced that she would be hosting a spiritual teacher at her home in a few days.

She described David LaChapelle as a seer, bard, storyteller, and healer. She said to me, "I think you'd love him. I hope you can come."

I had no desire to meet yet another teacher and felt tremendous resistance to going.

"Why do you like him?" I asked politely.

"Well, let me see . . . he has this gift for seeing each person's essence. Then he sometimes creates these spontaneous stories that reflect exactly the predicament you find yourself in; they are like your own personal myth and are both funny and deeply touching. He works with the group energy field to amplify everyone's connection to the Divine. He's a very accurate seer, and that seeing generates a field of trust and tenderness amongst people that were total strangers only moments before. It's hard to describe; you have to experience him.

"Oh, and by the way, he plays guitar and chants. And often he gives people homework assignments," she added.

"Homework assignments?"

"Yes, he looks at you and comes up with an antidote to your life predicament, and then when you do your assignment, your whole life changes!"

Hmm, I thought, not sure if I wanted to sign up for that.

I felt some reassurance when I read in David's bio that he had experienced a powerful Kundalini awakening while in his late teens, and that he had spent time in India with Swami Muktananda (a well-known guru). At least he knows what Kundalini is, I thought.

Curiosity aroused, I signed up for the upcoming weekend with David.

Homecoming

I arrived at Patricia's home a little late and joined the group already gathered in the large room that she used for our meditation circle. As I sat down, my eyes were drawn upward toward the ceiling, covered by a painted canvas depicting dramatic clouds and sky opening toward the light. It calmed the anxiety arising within me in anticipation of the day.

David sat on the floor, his lanky legs folded beneath him. I noticed his feet peeking out, covered in colorful socks. His straight grey hair fell in a disheveled manner across his piercing blue-grey eyes. A guitar sat cradled gently in his arms, and occasionally he strummed a few notes, which seemed to organize the energy in the room.

Unperturbed by my late arrival, he acknowledged me with a kind and welcoming glance. He greeted each newcomer with curiosity and delight, as if we were guests invited to his party. He made astute, often funny observations of each person, yet addressed them to the group at large, which quickly drew us into a web of intimacy.

His eyes rested upon me again. "What is your name?" he asked.

"Dani."

"Do you know the meaning of your name?"

"It's funny you would ask; I just looked it up. It comes from the root name Daniel, which I found out means 'God is my judge' in Hebrew."

"You have quite a strong connection to God and the Jewish ancestral line. Your crown chakra is wide open," he observed.

I immediately felt seen, relaxed, and safe.

David didn't seem to be in a rush to start the group; he patiently watched the energy in the room as it organically settled and people quieted down. He had no self-important urge to present "his" material; in fact, I would soon learn that we composed the material of his teachings!

He started to speak softly: "There is a profoundly deep intent to awaken embedded in all of us. How that happens is a mysterious process. I have noticed that group vibration opens and stabilizes portals to awakening. If the vibratory rate of the group is raised, then the rooting of our identity can come from a more essential state.

"Our ego function likes to think it can do this by itself. However, to stabilize awakening, you have to vibrate with something higher than your own frequency. Help comes from the world around you. There is something larger holding the polarity of our contractions.

"All of us are too contracted to hold the immensity of our true being. We have to find mitigating fields of kindness as we open."

I breathed deeply as he said this, thinking about how David framed the spiritual journey in such accessible language. The past few months, I had tried so hard to maintain my spiritual discipline and focus on my own. Being in a group with others once again allowed my loneliness and anxiety to go down a few more notches. I glanced around the room, and for a moment I ached for the familiar faces of my "Kabbalah" tribe. Leaving the school still felt like the wound of being newly divorced, and I hadn't yet established my life outside that community.

I didn't want a new community or a new teacher, yet the retreat with David nourished and grounded me. Despite my reservations, I began to attend his groups whenever he came to town. David called our group "Patricia's Suburban Posse," and we averaged around thirty or so people on any given day. We ranged from teenagers to elders in the community. All were given the same attentiveness and essential kindness, allowing us to feel safe and vulnerable without the fear of being judged.

The teenagers learned from the elders, and the elders learned from the teenagers. I imagine that this is how it used to be in tribal cultures. This was perfect for me in that I came to the group to break my patterns of isolation and balance my intense inner life in relationship to the outer world.

Gradually, I no longer felt like an alien from another planet just because of my inner Kundalini process.

David made himself available to all of us through emails and phone calls between visits. I reached out to him on a day when I felt particularly lonely and depressed and received one of his notorious "homework assignments" in response. He wrote:

Dani,

Thanks for the check-in.

Emotional imprints are among the hardest processes to move. It is most difficult to fight your way through the isolation at the emotional level.

If you reach from the contraction, the contraction becomes the reaching.

Because of your connection (to spirit), the work of surrender is on the inside. The emotional release won't move because it is a reflection of your fear of the inner.

So emotional isolation is a symptom of a spiritual resistance. The deep fear is that if you let go, you will be out of position with your fellow humans. Ironically, only by deep surrender do you come into correct position with your fellow humans.

A practice for you:

After meditating, walk a few blocks in Lambertville. Go into one shop after another and practice feeling the beings you meet as an expression of your meditation, not different than your meditation. Don't make an effort to relate. Simply abide in the arising of all beings.

If you lose your state, go back, meditate, and do the walk again.

Also find a school to volunteer for a few hours now and then. Nothing fancy, just being with lots of children.

Stay away from milk as if it were a plague.

Keep a fresh rose by your bedside and smell it upon waking and upon going to bed.

Contemplate the grains that grow around the planet. Visualize the sun entering the stream of grain formation and rising into golden nourishment.

Visualize this three times a day.

Be kind to yourself,

Be kind to yourself,

Be kind to yourself.

Love
David

I don't know how he knew about the milk; I never told him about being allergic to milk since birth. I also didn't tell him about the cheese and ice cream I had been regularly eating as comfort food, despite the resulting cramps in my belly.

I set out one morning to practice the walking meditation and had an extraordinary encounter that I will never forget.

I walked down to Main Street in Lambertville, toward my favorite coffee shop. Out of the corner of my eye, I could see the ochre and red robes of three Tibetan monks sitting on the bench in the front of the shop.

As I walked toward them, my client Gary approached from the opposite direction. He had been in my office the day before to receive healing as he went through treatment for liver cancer.

Now, Gary was not a spiritually oriented kind of guy, and in fact his liver cancer was most likely due to an over-indulgence of vodka. When I asked him what spiritual path he would be drawn to if he had a choice, he made a vague statement about Buddhism, because he didn't really believe in God.

So there was Gary, making a beeline for the coffee shop, arriving at exactly the same time as I did, both of us a bit stunned at seeing these elder Tibetan Buddhist monks in our little town of just barely eight thousand people. The youngest of the monks must have been seventy years old. The oldest must have been close to ninety. They didn't speak English, but there was an American woman with them acting as a translator.

One of them pointed to the bandage on Gary's arm from the chemo. The translator asked Gary about his illness and explained it to the monks. Two of the monks patted the bench, inviting Gary to sit down between them.

They each took one of Gary's hands and together chanted prayers for him in Sanskrit for over twenty minutes. By this time, I had tears streaming down my face. I don't know if Gary realized how unusual it was to have such a sacred opportunity for healing and blessing. He sat quietly on the bench and simply received their offering. Who could have arranged this perfectly timed meeting so filled with grace?

As much as the healing benefited Gary, my lesson that day was to understand that this is what it could be like to abide in unobstructed, compassionate relationship with my fellow human beings—miraculous!

To complete the other part of my assignment, I spent a few minutes every day visualizing myself as a seed that gradually grew into tiny shoots of grain, which then grew taller, nourished by the sun and the rain. I felt myself grow to full size and eventually fall to the earth as seed, completing the full cycle of growth and starting over again. This exercise helped me to rest in the unfolding stream of life. I viscerally felt my connection to the organic cycles and rhythms of life itself, very much like a continuously cycling Tree of Life.

I also put a large red rose in a vase by my bedside and luxuriated in its fragrance. I associated its smell with my dad, who often made vats of tea rose perfume for one of his main customers. As a child, this smell gave me a feeling of security and connection.

I never did find a way to work with young children.

I gradually became less and less isolated as I observed that all beings arise out of the same Oneness, and no matter how contracted they may seem in the moment, they are all in the process of awakening to their true nature. I began to practice tuning to a person's wholeness or essence before I noticed their problems. In this way, I could see how each person's life was an expression of wholeness, no matter what they had experienced: broken heart, loss, accident, or physical injury.

David taught me to watch the patterns of someone's preferred drama and to see the secondary lines of formation underneath them so that I could perceive what was trying to heal.

He said, "In every problem there is a higher soul quality that is actually trying to manifest. When you can accurately perceive this, you will have real wisdom. Whatever is truly seen will in time become true. A true perception is an energetic act that activates the energy of connection . . . it activates your potential because it's been seen."

I began to observe how relationships changed immediately when people relaxed into a field of acceptance and acknowledgement of their true nature. Healing happens organically when we are seen in this way.

During one retreat, David sat up front as usual, guitar in hand, watching the room like a professional tracker. He often picked the day's topic by rifling through our psyches to find the most pressing issues to bring up to the group.

His eyes landed right on me as he started to talk about the Jewish genetic line.

"The Jews are God's chosen people, and yet they have been wiped out again and again for the gifts they have. They were chosen to carry an extra vibration, a transmission of light given by God to Moses on Mt. Sinai. Genetically, they also carry a wiring embedded in fear from always having to move out of the line of danger. I see this fear in many of my Jewish acquaintances, this genetic fear of annihilation. It is a test of courage to put aside the fear of annihilation and place your trust in God.

"The remedy on an inner level is that you need to track through the fear to the brilliance of the Jewish line, rather than anchoring to the fear. If you consistently go to the fear, you become an anchor point for the fear."

I completely resonated with his words, as I was well acquainted with my "inner bag lady." For as long as I could remember, I had lived with an undercurrent of fear that had no rational basis. I think every Jew carries this fear in their genes from centuries of persecution and exile. The fear that I would run out of food or money or become homeless. In addition, every time I would prepare to teach a Kabbalah class, I had this irrational fear of being killed for misrepresenting the teachings. I knew this particular fear stemmed from a past life, but I hadn't been able to clear it.

David said, "Watch the structure, the shape of your anxiety, and anchor into the stream of light that is the becoming of all things. To heal a deep complex, you can't focus on the negative formation, because that only brings out the resistance."

When I anchored to the sense of this stream of light, my anxieties dissolved. However, deep-held ancestral traumas are also held collectively. We need a village to heal them. In David's groups, the group itself became the village. What happened next totally surprised me.

David's eyes moved toward my friend Michael. David focused somewhere above his head and commented: "I see your Jewish lineage going all the way back to the original twelve tribes of Israel."

Michael nodded. "My family were amongst the founding members of one of the oldest synagogues in Rhode Island, the Touro Synagogue."

David continued, "The Jewish lineage has a particular refinement in the ability to hold the frequency of the original emanation of light, undiminished. The Jewish religion contains texts of laws, rituals, behaviors, and ethics to create human bodies that could be vessels to hold that light. On the Jewish spiritual path, you have to turn to the lineage and embrace it so that the lineage itself will help you organize interiorly to hold the light and to 'burn correctly' so your interior 'vessels' don't shatter. We need to prepare ourselves to walk on holy ground.

"Now, allow yourself to gently open your crown and feel the presence of your ancestors."

Michael closed his eyes and focused on his crown. I perceived a shift in the energy around him, and my whole being started to vibrate in resonance to these Jewish presences that came to join him.

At that very moment, a ray of sunlight broke through the canopy of trees outside, passed through the living room window, and beamed directly into my Ajna chakra. I experienced this viscerally, as if skewered by a laser beam of light. Simultaneously, a piercing light entered my crown from above and spiraled down toward my heart like a corkscrew. As the light entered my heart chakra, I screamed—an earsplitting scream that I couldn't believe came out of my own mouth—as my heart exploded with the stored pain and trauma of my past lives within the Jewish lineage.

David, observing all of this and unperturbed, picked up his guitar and started to strum a soft chant in Hebrew, repeating the word *"shalom,"* which means peace. The group joined in, harmonizing, creating soft waves of peaceful currents. Gradually, my emotions quieted down.

Images of the life in which I had been exiled from my Jewish "tribe" paraded across my mind screen. I felt the anger I had against the elders who had thrown me out. I felt the strong inner resistance that I held toward the Jewish religion.

The beings asked me telepathically: "Are you ready to reconnect with us and the religion of your birth?"

This time, I answered: "Yes!"

I received their confirmation and acceptance in the form of more light, which flooded into my heart, flushing out lifetimes of karmic pain related to being Jewish.

That night, I awoke at two a.m. and meditated for a while. My brain and nervous system felt electrified with light, and a current of joy danced through my heart. I focused on a point of light that stayed on my mind screen when my eyes were closed.

I wrote Swamiji and Shivaji after this experience, and Swamiji commented, "Now you do all your practices according to the Tree of Life. The Jerusalem adepts are happy to accept you."

I reread the passage in *Kundalini Vidya* about the experience of "homecoming":

> Eventually there is usually a kind of homecoming, a connecting with the adepts of the lineage that one is affiliated with. It is an initiation, a spiritual connection, an entering, a communion. There is a sense of connectedness, a knowing of the presence of the spiritual guide, adept group, or spiritual tradition that is one's home.

Swamiji added, "Now your lineage is spiritual director to you. We are just the supporters."

16

Entry into No Self

Lambertville, New Jersey, 2005

As a result of these permutations [of Hebrew letters] your heart will become extremely warm, you will gain new knowledge that you never learned from human traditions nor derived from intellectual analysis. When you experience this, you are prepared to receive the shefa, the divine influx.

—Abraham Abulafia

After my homecoming experience, I had an irresistible urge to study Hebrew and explore Kabbalistic texts more deeply. Rabbi Sandy Roth appeared in my life as if sent by the angels above, and I began to meet with her weekly to study Hebrew.

Rabbi Sandy began her rabbinical studies after she already had a congregation. She had a passionate and deeply spiritual connection to Judaism. We became close friends, and our meetings together became a time of mutual spiritual inquiry.

Every time I left her office, Hebrew phrases circulated in my mind for hours.

The twenty-two letters of the Hebrew alphabet are said to be the basic creative/energy structures that give rise to the manifest world. In a similar way, the Sanskrit alphabet also presents each letter of the alphabet as a Divine force/sound. In the subtle body, each chakra has phonemes, letter sounds that are attributed to the various petals of the chakra. One can meditate on each sound, and the vibration will open the petals of the chakra. In Sanskrit, the sound vibration of the word OM is that which creates worlds and leads the student toward liberation.

In Kabbalah, wondrous powers have been associated with the Hebrew letters. Some Kabbalists even say that the Torah is not to be taken literally; rather it is actually a long string of letter codes that God literally used to bring the world into being.

Abraham Abulafia, a famous Kabbalist born in Spain in 1240, believed that by meditating with the Hebrew letters "one could gain knowledge of one's innermost self."

I started to experiment on my own, trying different meditations with the Hebrew letters that I found in Aryeh Kaplan's translation of the *Sefer Yetzirah*.

I approached these meditations cautiously because of the Kabbalistic tales warning of the danger of becoming ungrounded or going crazy when one practiced them by oneself. There is also the sixteenth-century legend of the *golem*, a form created by several rabbis who recited precise combinations of Hebrew letters that were said to produce an astral figure of a man. This figure was then animated by further placement of certain Hebrew letters. Supposedly, when alarm spread through the community at the appearance of the golem, it was destroyed by withdrawing those same Hebrew letters.

Contrary to the warnings on the danger of these meditations, I experienced no negative effects from my meditations; perhaps because I had already had years of spiritual practice under my belt and had already reached Makara.

I began by using the four-letter name of God, called the *Tetragrammaton*, as a focus for meditation.

I pronounced the names of the letters out loud—*Yod, Hei, Vav, Hei*—as I visualized them on my body: *Yod* at my head, *Hei* across my shoulders and down my arms, *Vav* down my spine, and the final *Hei* across my hips and down my legs. This practice filled my whole body with light and energy. The more I did the practice, the more my everyday egoic consciousness disappeared, and my sense of "I-ness" became absorbed in light and silence.

Then I added breath to my daily practice with the letters of the Tetragrammaton: I breathed in, visualizing the *Yod* in my head and breathed out as I visualized the first *Hei* across my shoulders and down my arms. I breathed in the *Vav*, and I visualized it running down along my spine, and I breathed out the second *Hei* as I visualized it across my hips and pelvis and moving down my legs. When I used breath and placed the letters in my body in this way, I felt simultaneously energized and very still. The letters merged into my body as pure vibration.

I shared my explorations with Swamiji, who had been reading many books on Kabbalah to be of service to his Jewish consultees. Swamiji then gave me additional Hebrew names of God to coordinate with the yoga postures in my Kundalini practice.

He said, "In Hebrew, as well as in Sanskrit, first God created light, then vibration, then sound, then letters, and finally words and names. When you chant the name of God, you bring light, vibration, and sound into your being."

The practice worked quite well, and I never experienced any conflict as the two traditions came together in my body.

One day, on Rabbi Sandy's recommendation, I took the train into New York City to visit the Jewish Theological Seminary library, where I spent hours looking at different Kabbalistic books.

In one obscure text, I came across a sentence that said something like: The ancient Jewish sages used to inscribe Hebrew letters and names of God on their robes so that they could be wrapped in the Divine name.

I received an immediate visual image as I read those words. I imagined prayer shawls inscribed with Hebrew names of God, and I decided I would attempt to paint my own shawls. First I needed to be even more familiar with the Hebrew alphabet. I bought a set of Hebrew alphabet cards and started to draw the shapes of the letters with a black marker on white paper. I became totally absorbed as I traced their curves and lines, and drawing them became a meditation in and of itself.

Then I decided to paint them. I wanted to paint their energy. As a trained artist, I thought it would be easy, and perhaps I could even exhibit the paintings when they were finished. I envisioned painting the letters, depicting them in such a manner that they would transmit their energy outward from the flat surface of the page.

I chose the mighty first letter of the Hebrew alphabet, *aleph*, as the first letter to paint. Our English word "alphabet" actually stems from a contraction of the first two Hebrew letters in the alphabet, aleph and bet. In Hebrew, the aleph is silent and has the numerical value of one. It represents unity and the indivisibility of God.

I started by painting a golden aleph floating in a sky of blue. As I worked to express the energy of the letter, the painting got darker and darker until all the light of the aleph became obscured in muddy dense colors. Unhappy with the results, I threw the painting in the trash can. The next day I started again, and the same thing happened. At the end of the day, I threw away another dark, muddy canvas.

I got more and more agitated as numerous attempts to paint this letter failed as it kept disappearing into darkness.

In despair, I sat down on my meditation cushion and prayed for help. I picked up *The Sefer Yetzirah* and, by chance, opened to page 91:

> At first, the initiate depicts the letter in transparent air, visualizing it clearly. . . . He then begins to see the letter as if he were looking at it through water . . . the letter begins to blur and fade as if it were being viewed through increasingly deep water . . . the initiate must then engrave and carve chaos and void, mire and clay. . . . At this stage, the form breaks up and dissolves completely. . . . Finally, all that is left is inky blackness, as if one were buried in totally opaque mud and clay. Later on, a fourth step returns the initiate to a state associated with fire and blinding light.

Astonished, I read this passage and understood my visual journey to the state of dissolution and nothingness. The stages of chaos, void, mire, and clay were expressed progressively as my paintings disappeared. The descent into no-thing-ness or no form that arose during the process of painting seemed to have been generated by the letter itself!

During my next consultation, I told Swamiji and Shivaji what I had been up to.

Swamiji said, "The 'aleph' is like Bindu in our tradition; it is the entry into monism, the experience of the One without the Second."

Shivaji elaborated, "The subtle experience of Bindu is an experience that is not an experience; if you can describe it as phenomenal experience, that isn't it. Bindu is beyond mind, words, and images. In fact, it is so unremarkable that it is not a nameable experience. Perhaps it can be compared to having the sensation of a period of lost time. You know something has happened, but you don't know what it is."

Initially, I didn't realize that the disappearing aleph marked my entry through the gateway of Bindu/Keter and into what PKYC calls "expanding process." My spiritual experiences were usually of the "bells and whistles" type, filled with light and spiritual beings. Bindu is the name for the point at the top of the head that is the culmination of Kundalini's journey to the pinnacle of the crown. To get there, Kundalini passes through a very subtle nadi, called Brahma nadi, that is akin to a thread passing through the eye of a needle. In the Tree of Life, Keter at the crown of the head is the parallel to Bindu.

The top of the head, or the fontanel, is the very spot that Jewish men cover with a yarmulke. In Sanskrit, "kapalah" means skull; the word sounds very similar to "Kabbalah," to receive. We receive the very highest teachings of nonduality through the movement of Kundalini through this very subtle Brahma nadi. When Kundalini passes through this nadi, the seeker experiences Oneness.

Earlier on my spiritual path, I had mistaken my vivid spiritual experiences as a sign of my advanced spiritual progress; however, as Shivaji later told me: "Until Kundalini progresses to Bindu, these experiences are not indicative of your spiritual progress. In fact, Zen teachers use the term *makyo*, 'ghost cave,' to describe the student's clinging to spiritual experiences and mistaking visions for enlightenment. All phenomenal experiences are still dualistic."

So, painting the letter aleph took me on an archetypal spiritual journey through darkness (represented by the mire and mud) to illumination. I did indeed paint the energy of the letter, but it didn't quite fit with my desire of a finished product.

Now I entered an extended period of time in my practice when my small sense of self repeatedly dissolved into the experience of no self, no body, no form, no namable experience. After years of visions, there was no-thing. Very anticlimactic.

This experience constituted a first step, a glimpse experience of ultimate reality. Some people have a big glimpse experience and don't return to the old view of the small, conditioned self. I had many years of "commuting" between the two before stabilization in Oneness emerged. Swamiji and Shivaji called this phase a plateau, an expanding process where one commutes between the Oneness experience and duality. Gradually, the experience of Oneness expands as one progresses.

The Kabbalists describe this oscillation as "running and returning to the place."

On the night of the full moon in March 2006, I had a significant dream that confirmed Kundalini's elevation to Bindu, the gateway to increasingly stable nondual awareness.

I dreamt that Swamiji came to get me in a car. When the car pulled up, I opened the door and hopped into the back seat. There was Swamiji, sitting next to Ramana Maharsi, the Indian master known for his spontaneous and complete nondual realization at the young age of sixteen. I looked into Ramana's eyes and received his darshan (spiritual initiation given by glance or touch). Then I looked into Swamiji's eyes and saw within them the same reflection of unconditioned luminosity. In fact, they looked like brothers in that moment.

When I awoke, I still felt this Divine transmission.

A day later, Shivaji sent out an email to everyone that said: "Swamiji has been in the South of India. He has been at his Great Master's mountain, near Arunachala, for the full moon night."

Arunachala is the mountain upon which Ramana Maharsi lived for all the years of his life! This was an unsolicited confirmation of my dream encounter.

Ramana Maharsi's presence in my dream confirmed that my spiritual practice had matured and that Kundalini Shakti had reached Bindu and beyond. I could now abide more often in the awareness of Oneness.

Only then, after I had experienced the Oneness/no-thing-ness that is the essence and source of the Hebrew letters, could I paint them while staying connected to both the worlds of form and formlessness.

I decided to continue my letter paintings on silk swatches in preparation for making the shawls. I didn't know how to paint on silk, but that didn't stop me. Again, the first results were disastrous, as I didn't know how to control the dyes, and all the colors spread into each other. I consulted a local artist, Juanita Yoder, known for the painted silk banners that graced some of our local churches. She gave me a few lessons in silk painting, and I went back to work.

I finished the first shawl, "Dancing Letters," after a few months of trial and error. Now I could wrap myself in all twenty-two Hebrew letters! I went on to create five more designs, with different Hebrew names of God or phrases from the psalms inscribed upon them. Eventually, I made them into *tallit*, the Jewish ritual prayer shawls. When people wear them, they report back to me that they can feel the shawls vibrate with the energy and vibration of the letters.

17

Freedom from the Body

January 2004

Death must die.

—Anandamayi Ma

Though I continued to have regular consultations with Swamiji and Shivaji, David LaChapelle also became a consistent guide in my life.

By now I trusted David enough to sign up for an extended retreat on the Big Island of Hawaii in February. The retreat would be held on a private permaculture farm, where we would be "glamping"—camping with the luxury of a kitchen, a bathroom, showers, and a yurt for our meetings. I couldn't wait to get out of the cold East Coast weather and explore the beaches and sacred sites of Hawaii.

Two weeks before the retreat started, on a cold crisp January day, I got into my car at twelve noon to drive to a neighboring town to lead my monthly supervision group for healers. This group remained the last teaching connection I had with ASOS. While driving, I contemplated the fact that in a few months this group would end, and

I would have no more active ties to the school. I felt sad but also had faith that my inner connection to the Divine would lead me forward.

It had snowed the night before, but the roads were clear. I maneuvered the car through the narrow streets lined with piles of snow and turned onto a country road, heading toward Princeton, New Jersey. Random thoughts passed through my mind as I cruised along at forty mph.

Although this road had been plowed, high snow banks lined its sides, encroaching on the driving lanes. What I couldn't see was the treacherous black ice that lay beneath the snow.

The last thing I remember is a strange pulling sensation in my hands as they instinctively gripped the steering wheel.

The next thing I remember is watching myself from above my body as I joked with a man who sat in the passenger seat of my car. Somehow, I talked to this man through my body, while my consciousness was above my body.

I was in the most peaceful and relaxed state I have ever experienced. I had no identification with the current life and body of "Dani"; only pure conscious awareness was present. The senses of time, duty, future planning, and purpose were absent. I felt a freedom and joy I had never experienced.

Moments later, I slipped back into my body, like a hand entering a glove, a very small and tight glove.

I stopped joking with the man midsentence.

My brain clicked "on," and immediately I thought: There's a man in my car! How did he get here? Why is he in my car?

I found my voice and asked out loud, "Who are you, and what are you doing in my car?"

He said, "Don't move, you have been in a car accident; the ambulance is on the way."

"What do you mean, I've been in an accident?"

"Look at your car."

My eyes looked outward, and I panicked. The windshield looked like cracked marbles, and glass and debris covered the front of the dashboard. The air bags hadn't gone off.

I quickly wiggled my toes and fingers. They worked! I breathed a sigh of relief. At least I wasn't paralyzed. I looked out again. The car rested upright in a field, and the road was nowhere in sight.

"Where were you headed?" he asked. "Is there someone I can call?"

"I-I don't know . . . ," I said with growing alarm. I couldn't pull up the data from my brain.

I heard voices approaching the car. "Stay still, we are going to cut you out of there."

Within minutes, I lay flat on a stretcher. I closed my eyes, unable to compute the whole situation as I was carried what seemed to be quite a distance to the ambulance waiting on the road. Inside the ambulance, the EMTs cut my clothes right down the center of my body, through my favorite ski jacket, my shirt, and my bra. They quickly attached equipment to monitor my vital signs. I closed my eyes again and floated upward. I felt so alone, out of control, and scared.

At the hospital, I waited on the stretcher in the hall until they could get me in for a CAT scan and MRI. By then I had remembered my name and started to recover some short-term memory. I found my purse and my cell phone. I remembered that it was Ellen's house I had been driving toward and called her. Over an hour had passed.

She picked up immediately. "Where are you? Are you okay? We are all sitting here, leading the group ourselves."

"I had a car accident. I am in the hospital waiting for the results of my scans," I answered, in tears as I said the words.

"What hospital did they take you to?"

"I am in Trenton," I said.

"Sandra and I are coming to get you," Ellen replied.

I didn't argue. Relief flooded my body, as I had no relatives nearby. I also remembered that Sandra was a nurse. Thirty minutes later, they appeared by my side like two ministering angels, just as I was being released from the hospital.

"Hi," I said. "The scans showed no damage to my neck. I have a concussion and one small scratch on my body."

Sandra took off her winter coat and wrapped it around me over the hospital gown. They ushered me into her car and brought me home. I called my friend Beth, who agreed to stay with me overnight to monitor the concussion.

When I arrived home, I glanced around. The morning dishes sat in the sink just as I had left them, as if nothing had happened. I climbed upstairs and crawled into bed, assuring Sandra and Ellen that I would stay still until Beth arrived.

I called my parents, brother, and sister. They asked a million questions about the accident, and I could barely form answers to their questions. Mostly they were relieved that I was unharmed. I also called the PKYC office, left a message about the accident, and asked Shivaji to inform Swamiji.

That evening as I drifted in and out of sleep, I once again saw the flash of an orange robe at my feet. I waved at the ephemeral vision, feeling great comfort, knowing that Swamiji had checked in on me. Although outwardly fine, my brain didn't work quite right for over a month. Weird electrical impulses flitted through my left temporal lobe. It felt like a short in the wires.

About a week after the accident, I rented a car and drove to the site where my car had been towed. There sat my crumpled Saturn, my first car, bought at age forty, as I left New York City to move to New Jersey. I opened the undamaged passenger door to collect my personal belongings. Everything from the back of the car had been thrown forward, and glass from the shattered windshield covered the seat.

Then, looking down, I gasped!

There on the front seat, in pristine condition, my address book lay open to a picture of Swamiji that I always carried with me. His intense eyes blazed outward. I knew in that moment that I had been protected and had survived by the grace of a higher power.

I called the police and requested a copy of the police report. Strange to read the clinical description of the middle-aged woman—me—taken from the scene of a car crash by ambulance. I noticed the phone number of the man who had witnessed the accident and sat with me in the car. I immediately called him to thank him.

"I am the girl who you helped in the car accident last week. I wanted to thank you and ask you, how did you come to be in the car with me?"

"I was driving in the oncoming lane, and I saw your car go out of control. You must have hit black ice. At first, I thought you were headed straight toward me. But then your car veered right toward the field. It launched sideways into the air, flew over a pile of snow, flipped a few times in the air, and landed upright in the field. It flew over a fire hydrant and between two telephone poles. If you had hit either one of them, I am sure you would have been killed instantly. I pulled over and ran into the field to see if you were okay."

I felt dizzy as he described the accident. How could I not remember any of this happening? I must have hit my head and left my body the minute the car went out of control.

"I can't thank you enough for being there. You were my angel. I wasn't all alone, and I am so grateful you called the ambulance."

He graciously responded, "Anyone would have done the same."

I walked about with a newfound appreciation for my physical body. I marveled that it worked, that I could walk and talk, that I was alive. My not-so-skinny thighs, my freckles, and my unruly hair ceased to be a focus of my scrutiny. However, I still felt as if I floated a couple of feet above my body, not fully inhabiting it.

Although I didn't go through a tunnel of light, I knew that I'd had a near-death experience. My relationship to life itself changed. I had experienced the "peace that passeth all understanding" mentioned in Philippians 4:7.

I knew for sure that consciousness continues beyond death and that "I" was not my body. I knew for sure that "I" was not defined by my circumstances, my career, or my possessions. I marveled at the miraculous gift of life itself, and I felt determined to live out the rest of my time in this body with joy and inner freedom. I could visualize the whole shape of my life, the way the astronauts could see the whole shape of the earth from the moon. I started to make new decisions from this larger vantage point. I felt fearless.

I emailed David about the accident, wondering if I should still attend the retreat.

He replied, "Dani, it looks as if you have hit the reset button in your life. This is a turning point. Come to Hawaii; it will be good for you in this time of transition."

I assembled the camping gear and made the arrangements to fly to Hawaii. After ten hours in the air, as the plane circled the Kona airport for more than half an hour, I got woozy and nauseous; the body memory of rotating through the air when the car flew out of control got triggered by the airplane's movements.

Finally, the plane landed, and I walked out into the warm Hawaiian air, scented with plumeria blossoms. I spotted David by the baggage claim. He took one look at me and gently put his hand on my lower spine. He stood with me, right there in the middle of the hustle and bustle of the airport, until my soul came down from the clouds and returned once again to my body.

We stopped at the ocean for a quick swim, and I felt immediately soothed by the embrace of the warm Pacific waters as my nervous system thawed from its frozen state.

"Dani," David said, "tomorrow we are going to bury your body in the sand. Pele, the Great Mother of the Big Island, will heal you."

So the next day, my friends dug a shallow trench in the sand; I lay down, and they covered me with sand up to my neck. Just my just head stuck out, and they draped it with a towel so I wouldn't burn. While they frolicked in the water, I stayed still, eyes closed, feeling the vibration and pulse of the land beneath me. They unpacked me an hour later, and I felt more connected to myself.

I fell in love with the Big Island and returned for two more retreats with David. It opened my eyes to the possibility that I might not want to spend the rest of my life in New Jersey. Maybe I will move to Hawaii and live the rest of my life in paradise, I thought.

I first decided I would explore living in California, as I couldn't really envision working and supporting myself from a small island in the middle of the ocean. It felt too far away from family and friends. My brother lived in San Francisco, and on my way back from a trip to Hawaii, I asked him to show me his favorite towns in Northern California.

We did a grand tour of Mill Valley, Marin, Petaluma, Sebastopol, Santa Rosa, and Napa. On that trip, I felt my soul start to root itself to the West Coast. After spending a magical afternoon with two friends under a huge tree in a Napa park, I went home and put my house in Lambertville up for sale. It sold seven months later, just a few months before the big housing-market crash in 2007.

The profit I made enabled me to embark on my new phase of life with a small nest egg. I held a garage sale that shrank my possessions down to a movable size and booked flights for myself and Bindu, my cat.

A dear friend generously offered lodging in a plush log cabin on his beautiful ranch and vineyard in Calistoga until I found my own place. Thus, my West Coast life began.

I could not have imagined it would take me seven years and three moves before I finally found home in the paradise that is Santa Barbara. Nor could I imagine that my joy in discovering the incredible beauty of California would be offset by a series of devastating losses.

18

India: A Second Homecoming

Rishikesh, India, 2009

One day, Shivaji called me and announced: "Dani, Swamiji has invited you to come to a retreat in India!"

My heart leapt with joy. I had been on the waiting list for this trip for two years. Each year, Swamiji invited just a few students to travel to his home in Rishikesh to spend almost a month on retreat with him. I immediately said yes, grateful that I had the money from my house sale to fund the trip.

In February 2009, I flew to Newark airport where I joined three other PKYC consultees for the long flight to New Delhi. Our flight landed at eleven p.m. India time, and Swamiji and Shivaji were waiting for us right outside the gate. They had driven six hours from Rishikesh to formally greet us at the airport.

My eyes teared up as Swamiji stood in front of each of us and grasped each of our hands in formal greeting. He then silently placed orange "Om" shawls around our necks. I hadn't seen him in over six years, because for that period of time, he had lost his US visa. Once again,

I felt stunned by the emanation of sanctity and serious-ness that surrounded him.

We rested overnight in a hotel in New Delhi. The next day, we piled into cars that we nicknamed the *Om mobiles* (two white taxis with big Om stickers pasted on the back windshields), and we headed north to Rishikesh, a town that sits along the Ganges River in the foothills of the Himalayas. It is a known for its ashrams, temples, and holy sites and is a magnet for spiritual seekers.

Swamiji's apartment complex sat a few hundred feet in from the banks of the holy river, almost directly across from the now-abandoned ashram where the Beatles received initiation into Transcendental Meditation from Maharishi Mahesh Yogi.

Swamiji rented several apartments right next to his quarters for retreat guests. I settled into a two-bedroom apartment that I shared with my roommate, Valerie, for the next three weeks. Right up the river sat the Sivananda Ashram, started by the renowned Swami Sivananda, who considered Swamiji a colleague and consulted with him. Valerie gracefully volunteered to take the bedroom outfitted with the Indian style squat toilet bathroom, because the room had a terrace. I chose the room with a real Western toilet. Both of us were happy with the arrangement and settled in.

The next morning after breakfast, Swamiji and Shi-vaji came into my room for my first consult. I expected that he would reprimand me for my lapsed spiritual prac-tice. With all the changes in my life, I hadn't been doing my practice as regularly as I had in the past.

Instead, he introduced me to Sunita, a pleasant-faced young Indian woman.

Swamiji declared, "You will receive an Ayurvedic massage every other day from Sunita. Your body is off center." (Who wouldn't be off center after sitting for twenty-two hours in an airplane?)

"Your right and left sides are crisscrossed energetically; there's a block in your neck, and energy can't flow down into your body."

He pointed to my legs and calves and said, "Pull up your pants legs."

He had Sunita watch as he demonstrated, "Massage her muscles this way." He then squeezed the muscles of my calves with vigor! I blushed as he demonstrated the proper pressure on my leg. He's a monk after all and usually didn't touch women!

Later in the morning, Sunita covered my bed with layers of sheets. She heated specially prepared Ayurvedic oil in a small pan, then slathered the warm oil all over my head and naked body. *Abhyanga* (Ayurvedic massage) is done with smooth long strokes, and the oils remove toxins from the body. With the luxury of a massage every other day, the chronic tension in my body began to gradually disappear.

Two days later, Swamiji and Shivaji again came into my room, and I received a grim analysis of my spiritual progress.

Swamiji pronounced, "Her process is not improving because she has not been doing her regular practice due to fear. She has lost hope and self-confidence. The light from Keter is there, but it is not coming through the heart down the central column to Malchut. Her heart is broken. She feels she needs someone (a man) to be responsible for her. Her female brain is suppressed by her male brain. It's as if the male says, 'You work for me, then I am responsible for you.'

"But the female part has no idea she should be responsible for herself and not be dependent on anyone else. The real unity is with the Divine within. We all have male and female within us. When you have a good heart connection, then you can never be alone. All the saints feel that their own soul is their true beloved. When you have great devotion, it makes the two become one."

He continued with his appraisal of my process: "Her sexual creative center in the Tree of Life, Yesod, is not good. The patterns of abuse at the hands of men have caused strong damage in this center. The repair job is not well done because of the irregularity of her practice."

"What should my practice be, Swamiji? I stopped doing the old one because it didn't feel effective anymore."

"Wait, and we'll see," he said.

There was no pushing Swamiji. He operated on "Indian" time, which meant no rush, no push.

On my third night in India, the night of the full moon, I had an intense lucid dream. I found myself in the presence of many masters. One of them touched me with a rod of some sort, and the crown of my head became electrified. Electricity descended forcefully through my spine and woke me up. I heard myself saying the word "Yes!" out loud, as I confirmed an oath to an initiation I didn't fully remember. I awoke completely, still electrified and somewhat stunned.

A few days later, when I had the opportunity to tell Swamiji about my full moon–initiation dream, he said, "Yes," as if he already knew about it, then added, "No problem with Keter." That's all he said. He never fed our egos, but he always wanted to hear about our inner experiences.

After the dream, the days in India settled into a regular schedule of meditation practice, meals, afternoon class with Swamiji, and outings to spiritual sites. We visited the ashram of the deceased saint Anandamayi Ma, known as the bliss-intoxicated mother. Her body was interred in Kankhal, a neighboring town, where I felt her living spirit bestow blessings and grace upon all of us as we meditated at her shrine.

Every morning after practice and breakfast, Valerie and I went out together and walked for two hours on the banks of the Ganges. We walked across the four-hundred-and-fifty-foot-long suspension bridge that crossed the river from Rishikesh to the jewel-like town of Lakshman Jhula, a bustling tourist town, where it is said that Lakshmana from the Ramayana once crossed the Ganges on a jute rope.

We immersed ourselves in the sights and smells of daily Indian life: the cows, the monkeys, the families living in tents, the laundry drying on the rocks, the gypsies with horses and pigs, the vendors, the beggars, the motorbikes with whole families aboard, and the *sadhus* bathing on the ghats. I never tired of it. No matter how crazy it all appeared on the outside, the underlying reverence for God permeated all of Indian life. Altars to deities appeared in roadside niches and before the entrances of the most humble of homes. Everywhere, Sanskrit chanting pervaded the atmosphere, acting as a soundtrack for the panorama of human experience before us.

One night, close to the end of our trip, I again had a lucid-dream experience. At first, I found myself in a nondescript dream scene, then all of a sudden within the dream, a window frame appeared, kind of like a TV. I entered the window, and the scene before me came alive in a three-dimensional way. I found myself vividly living in one of my past lives:

Two men, named Darba and Ecarta, came into the room where I sat at a table, two dogs lying at my feet. The men let me know they had come to kill me. I had the sense that we were Essenes. I had somehow challenged them ethically by telling the truth to the community. They made me break my vegetarian diet by eating some chicken before they hauled me off. They first tried to strangle me, then they hung me up to die. I recognized one of the men who had come to take me away as someone in my current life. I felt despair, hopelessness, and rage at the men as they dragged me from my home to be murdered. I also felt betrayed by the hypocrisy within the community itself, which didn't come to my defense.

I awoke in terror, my heart beating rapidly. After the dream, I couldn't sleep and my mind was agitated. I felt so much hatred for those men and the Jewish authorities, and I reflected on how that current of hatred ran through my life in the present time.

When I told Swamiji about it the next day, he commented on the dream, "Your death by murder in this past life made you feel hopeless. You told the real truth, and therefore you became a problem to them. In your current and past lives, you were used by the false promises of men, who said to you: 'I'll make your life better.' But the real promise is from God, and a real guru will make you the *same or better as he is and not abuse or use you!*"

I had never heard any of my other teachers say: "I will make you the same as or better than I am"—there always seemed to be a power differential, with the implication that I could never reach the level of the teacher.

Going Home

The rest of our time in India passed quickly.

One day, our little group walked together with Swamiji and Shivaji over the bridge to Lakshman Juhla. We encountered a young Chabad rabbi stationed in Rishikesh.

Swamiji approached him, offering his hand, and said, "*Shalom.*"

I watched them chat, Swamiji in his long orange robe and the rabbi in his long black garments. I noticed Swamiji pointing at me, and both nodded their heads.

He must have told the rabbi I was Jewish, because when they parted, Swamiji strode over to me and said, "You will go to celebrate *Shabbat* this Friday evening at the rabbi's home, which is also his synagogue."

I didn't argue, curious about experiencing a Jewish Shabbat in India.

When Friday night approached, Swamiji sent me off in the Om mobile with his driver. The driver waited outside for two hours while I went into a garden courtyard for the Shabbat meal and service. I found myself amongst a few adult tourists and some young Israeli kids just out of the army, looking for a good meal. The young rabbi gave a lovely talk, and afterward we feasted on hummus, Mediterranean salads, and *challah* (bread served on Shabbat)—all washed down with vodka for those who drank!

The rabbi invited Swamiji and Shivaji for a visit on Sunday. When Sunday arrived, all of us went back to the *Beit Chabad* (Chabad house) and entered the courtyard and sat for tea with the rabbi. His five or six kids were running around, and his wife served us, then disappeared.

After some small talk about the Hindu and Jewish traditions, the rabbi shared, "For some years, I became fixated on the 'other side,' or what some call 'evil,' and

I could not believe that it really existed. Then a friend convinced me it did indeed exist. I came to believe that the Jewish people have a special mission to preserve the 'good side' and uphold the light."

Swamiji said, "Yes, we each have different gifts or talents, each according to their karma. See what is given to you by God, and pray for help to manifest it. The problem comes if you believe that your way is the only way or that your people are the only ones."

Swamiji then shared case stories with the rabbi about his consultees who, though they weren't Jewish, had Jewish souls and memories of Jewish past lives. One such person remembered dying at Masada, and the other remembered dying in the Holocaust. They talked for a while longer and ended their discussion with Swamiji telling the rabbi that he wanted to learn Hebrew and the rabbi sharing a book with him. They shook hands warmly, and we all piled back into the waiting cars.

At this point, we had three days remaining on retreat. Shivaji had noticed that, in the past, Swamiji always withdrew his attention and went inward a few days before a group departed for home, and she decided to say something to Swamiji about it.

Swamiji's response to her comment manifested two days before we were to leave. Perhaps to teach Shivaji a lesson, he didn't leave the dining table from after breakfast at nine a.m. until ten p.m. at night. Since Swamiji didn't leave the dining table, we didn't leave the dining table. We sat there through three meals, and for thirteen hours, he regaled us with stories from his "cases," his early years as a teacher, and his wandering years as a mendicant. He certainly was on a roll. The stories were fascinating, and the energy was intense! I sat to his immediate right and felt as if I were immersed in a roiling cauldron of energy.

One particular story that Swamiji related from his wandering days stands out in my mind:

"I stopped to rest in Goa after a long day of walking. It was already dark when I found a wood platform in the middle of a forest. I lay down, and I went to sleep hungry.

"In the middle of the night, I awoke to see a monk before me with a lantern and a plate of food! I said to him, 'How did you find me here? How did you know I was hungry?'

"The monk answered, 'My dead master appeared to me. My master said, "Go bring food to this monk who is sleeping at the site of my Mahasamadhi shrine (burial site)."'

"The monk thanked me for choosing this special place to rest, because it enabled him to have a vision of his deceased master!"

Swamiji exclaimed, "Can you believe that? It really happened!"

When the time came to depart India, we again climbed into the two Om mobiles for the return trip to New Dehli. We stayed overnight at a hotel, and the next day planned a visit to *Akshardam*, a kind of cultural theme park dedicated to the history and saints of India.

That night, I sat in bed reading the book *Death Must Die*, which is the journal of Atmananda, edited by Ram Alexander, an Austrian woman who became a lifelong disciple of Anandamayi Ma, whose ashram we had visited.

I stared at the picture of the radiant Anandamayi Ma, trying to imagine what it would have been like to know her.

Suddenly, it felt as if the crown of my head cracked open, and I started sobbing as light flooded into my brain.

It kept flooding and flooding in, and I went into a state of bliss. Tears came as the deluge of light released more old, stored-up pain in my heart. I could barely tolerate it, and at one point I wondered who had initiated this downpour. At that moment, I sensed Swamiji's presence and the presence of the Jewish adepts around me.

As my consciousness dissolved into the download of light, I could hear a cacophony of loud, boisterous music right outside my window. A wedding procession marched its way down the street, accompanying the Divine deluge happening inside me. I laughed at this Divine coincidence.

The downflow lasted about half an hour, and when the energy subsided, all I could do was lie down and fall asleep. I had never experienced an opening of this magnitude. What has just happened? I wondered with amazement.

The next day, as we toured Akshardam, I could barely walk or focus. Swamiji noticed but remained silent. By the evening meal, I started to come back to my normal sense of self, and then it was time to depart.

We got back in the cars and headed to the airport. I happened to sit in the same car as Swamiji and Shivaji. I sat up front with the driver, and they sat together in the back. Swamiji went inward, and I felt drawn into deep meditation as his state of *Nirvikalpa samadhi* (Absorption in the One) permeated the car. The twenty-two-hour trip home felt painless as I basked in the afterglow of this experience.

It took me a year to ask Swamiji what had happened that night.

Swamiji simply commented, "You've been accepted back by the adepts of your lineage." From his comment, I understood that I'd had a second "homecoming experience"—five years after the first one that took place in David LaChapelle's group in Princeton.

I asked, "How can I have more contact with these adepts and get to know them better?"

"It's not possible to know them with your mind; you can't create that contact with your will or your ordinary consciousness. They will come to you. Make your life simple; become a monastery of one. Make your physical self strong and your life good."

I have come to realize that these adepts are the holders of the hidden knowledge of the Jewish way to self-realization, the Kabbalah. Their guidance is subtle and not in words; rather, they seed important concepts that eventually filter down to my daily reality. I feel them overseeing things from a distance, especially as I write this book.

Who am I to have this connection? I don't know. All I do know is that the longing for God is a holy longing—it is the ultimate longing—and this longing is always seen and acknowledged by the adepts who help humankind evolve. Each spiritual path has spiritual adepts who oversee their lineage, and when our longing for God gets strong enough, they guide us step by step on our path, through the channels of spirituality that are most familiar to our souls, toward liberation. Even the most circuitous paths lead home.

19

Befriending the Angel of Death

California, 2009–2013

Life is short. It can come and go like a feather in the wind.

—Shania Twain

Death became my teacher and took up camp in my life from 2009 to 2013, during which time I experienced six staggering losses.

The path of death illuminates our purpose in life, which is to know the Creator as pure, unconditional *love* while alive, right *now*, not waiting till we are at death's door or for the afterlife. Walking with death on my shoulder has become the norm since this time.

Becoming friends with death finished the lesson that the Hebrew letter aleph began: *How to stay present in the face of chaos, disintegration, and loss of form.* Knowing that all of us are so much vaster than our body or circumstances in life. Life is continuous; death is just a change of clothes.

Walking with death put everything in my life into focus. The awareness of the shortness of life made me keenly aware of living with impeccability. Each loss in my life became an encounter with the Great Mystery. I questioned: How do we make sense of life? Where do we go when we die? Does life continue? I observed that we die the way we have lived, and it is better to prepare for the moment of death now by living with impeccability, for we never know which day will be our last.

- David LaChapelle died of throat cancer on July 21, 2009.

- Rabbi Sandy Roth died of cancer on March 8, 2011.

- My beloved cat Bindu died on August 23, 2011.

- Kathryn Cameron, my dear friend, died of cancer on August 29, 2012.

- My mother, Sandra Antman, died of complications due to Alzheimer's disease on April 20, 2013.

- My father, Abe Antman, died of complications due to heart failure on April 23, 2013, just two days after my mother.

How odd to see the date of death beside the name of someone you have known and loved, imagining the date of your own death, placed next to your own name, as you calculate the amount of time you have left.

What would you do if you knew your exact time and date of death? Would it make a difference? Would you simply watch the seconds, minutes, and hours slip away, like sand slipping through an hourglass? Would you become fearless? Fearful? Risk a declaration of love? Leave an abusive situation? Create a legacy? Complete your bucket list? Or change nothing at all?

Bindu

Bindu, my cat, had a fatal seizure right in front of me, and I watched helplessly, unable to pick her up to take her to a vet. Seconds before her seizure, we shared an unforgettable moment: she came very close, put her paws on my chest, and said goodbye, soul to soul. But I didn't expect the end to come so quickly.

When the seizing stopped, I put her in the carrier, but I saw she was barely breathing. I took her to the emergency animal hospital, where all they could do was give her the lethal injection. It was clear to me that her soul had left her body earlier. For months afterward, I sensed her presence in the house, watching me from her favorite position on the bed. I grieved for her as if I had lost a child. Losing her broke my heart open.

I will never forget her pink bunny ears, her loud snoring, her snuggles under the covers by my feet, and seeing her run all over my apartment with her head stuck in a boot.

David LaChapelle

In March 2008, David received the diagnosis of stage four throat cancer. He'd had a growth on his neck for several months before he finally went for a biopsy. David? Throat cancer? It seemed impossible. Beloved by so many, his mission as a teacher had just started to blossom. His life was in service to so many beings. How could he have cancer?

David wrote an email to the community after receiving his diagnosis:

The condition must have been present for a considerable time beforehand, but I thought it was a result of Lyme disease. There is a stunning dichotomy between the health of the body and a deeper state of being, when a life-threatening disease manifests. Interestingly from the moment of diagnosis a deep and abiding sense of calm and well-being has arisen spontaneously within me.

This has been invaluable in taking me through much physical pain and discomfort. I attribute this sense of well-being to the fruits of my intense spiritual work during this lifetime, and it points to a state of fundamental well-being that is not conditioned by the body.

I remember that my Kabbalistic healing teacher, Jason Shulman, used to say that "cancer is a community of cells that are out of relationship with each other," since cancer cells reproduce faster than what is normal or needed. The healing of cancer, therefore, has to do with the balancing of a fundamental aspect of relationship.

Although it is hard to pinpoint any one causal agent with cancer, so often in my cancer patients, I see a failure in early nurturing that creates a profound hunger for love. It's as if the cells themselves are in a state of agitation and deprivation, so perhaps they over-reproduce to compensate for this lack. Cancer patients are often amazing givers and healers, giving to others what they themselves didn't receive. This creates an energetic imbalance in the body. Unfortunately, by the time cancer is physically manifest, it is so aggressive that even if the original emotional wound is healed, the healing of the body doesn't always follow.

David fought for his life with the utter conviction that he could heal his cancer by natural means. It takes a village to support someone dealing with aggressive cancer treatment. The community supported his healing journey, chanted with him, and witnessed his process. We joined him in the hope that each new remedy he tried would be the one that kicked the scourge of cancer out of his body.

He tried an exclusive alternative healing clinic in Switzerland, cooked herbs, imbibed folk remedies, and went to healers and psychics. I had a dream shortly after his diagnosis in which I saw his partner, Ananda, arrive at our group gathering in Princeton. She looked older and more mature than her current age. She entered the room alone, without David. In that moment, I knew with an inner conviction that David wouldn't make it. Still, I held out hope that I was wrong.

Cancer is a worthy opponent, and facing it head on is probably the greatest accelerator of spiritual growth that I have ever seen. David considered cancer a force that ripened his soul and a condition that for some reason grace had bestowed upon him to help him mature his self-realization.

He often quoted Ramana Maharshi, who'd had cancer at the end of his life. Ramana wrote:

The self is neither born nor dies, neither grows nor decays, nor does it suffer any change. When a pot is broken, the space within it is not, and similarly, when the body dies, the Self in it remains eternal.

David stayed aligned with his true Self throughout his journey.

About a year after his diagnosis, David told me that the Angel of Death came for him, and he told him to go away! It must have worked, because he didn't die until a year after his appearance, two years after being diagnosed with throat cancer. I didn't know you could negotiate with the Angel of Death. I filed away this interesting piece of information in the event that I should ever need it.

David's creativity exploded, even as he was confined to his bed. He sent us a constant stream of emails that illuminated his inner process. He created luminous Photoshop collages accompanied by quotes from the Jewish mystical text of the Zohar. Later, he made hundreds of pencil drawings, which he paired with poems and quotes from spiritual sources. This river of creativity seemed to come from the Source itself.

In mid-July 2009, I received a clear inner message that it was time to visit him, if I wanted to see him before he died. It felt urgent, so I booked a flight to Durango, Colorado, where David and Ananda had rented a place in town so that David could have easier access to medical care.

After chatting with Ananda for a bit, I went upstairs to see David. He looked horrible. He had aged twenty years since I had last seen him, and his face was haggard; however, his eyes burned as sharp and bright as always. The tumor on the side of his throat had grown to the size of a golf ball, and he had finally accepted intravenous pain relief.

I sat on the corner of the bed. "Can I do anything to make you more comfortable?" I asked.

"Could you massage my feet? It helps take my mind off the pain," he said.

As I massaged his feet, he dozed off, with his hands still resting on the keyboard of his ever-present laptop. Just then, I felt a subtle movement above my head, as if an invisible curtain had parted. I sensed a group of light beings gathering around him, joyously preparing to celebrate his imminent arrival.

"What was that?" David asked, suddenly awake, as he felt the shift of energy in the room.

"You are surrounded by light beings. You know you could stop fighting now," I said softly. "You could just surrender."

"Hmmpf," he muttered and went back to his computer.

A book about the Brazilian faith healer John of God lay open on the bed.

"Do you like him?" I asked.

"I am thinking of going to Brazil to see him. Someone has already brought him my picture, and I am receiving distant healings from him."

I couldn't imagine David getting on a plane in his frail condition and making the long trip to Brazil. However, I could see that thinking about visiting John of God gave him hope, and he still had some fight left in him.

Ananda went home to their house in Silverton for the night to get some much-needed rest. Two of us, myself and another friend, Ron, were left in charge of David's care. That night, David's pain levels increased. In addition to the pain from the tumor, he had abdominal pain because he hadn't had a bowel movement in over a week. He seemed to be going downhill fast. I was scared, and I didn't want him to die on my watch. Ananda should be here, I thought, it wouldn't be right for him to pass while she's away. Feeling intense anxiety, I said, "I think we should take you to the hospital."

David, who never raised his voice, screamed at me: "I will not go to the hospital! If I go to the hospital, they will kill me!"

Ron gave him an enema, which, thank God, I didn't have to administer. Eventually, he fell asleep. Ananda returned the next morning, and I flew home that evening, knowing that I would never see David again.

It turns out that David's words were prophetic. The next morning, Ananda took him to the hospital for a prearranged appointment. While on the exam table, his breathing changed dramatically. A short time later, he left his body like the yogis do, on the wings of the breath. He died in the hospital, just as he had feared.

Earlier that morning, before he'd gone to the hospital, he sent what turned out to be his last email and drawing.

He wrote:

I have journeyed to the edge of life and death and back. Clearly, a new chapter in my life. I am wiped clean by this journey. I am in considerable pain . . . and I await whatever new instructions there are for me.

Many blessings to you, may you treasure each moment of each day, for it can change dramatically, when you least expect it.

And then just a few hours later, he was gone. These words haunt me and inspire me to make the most of each day and treasure the blessings that I already have. Like David, I watch carefully for the openings, the signs and omens that guide me from above. I no longer push my way through life with my will. I wait patiently, or almost patiently (not my best quality), for the right moment to move ahead or to slow down, watching for the cues from the fabric of life itself to guide my way, knowing that everything has its season, its cycle.

Kathryn

Around the same time that David was ill, one of my soul sisters and closest of friends, Kathryn Cameron, was diagnosed with bone cancer after having been in remission from breast cancer for several years. She had just moved to Santa Barbara from the East Coast, a year after I had settled in Sebastopol, in Northern California. As her health deteriorated, I moved to Santa Barbara to be there for her as she went through treatment.

I became part of a group of close friends who cared for her through her illness. We accompanied her through radiation, relentless pain, and physical fragility. I often imagined that some time long ago, in another life, we were together in a royal court, where she was the generous queen, and I served her with a sense of loyalty and admiration, not subservience.

Cancer wore her down, yet her soul burned brighter than ever. She bore her discomfort with the same kind of "royal" grace with which she lived her life. Sometimes I would awake in the middle of the night, in my own house, and sense that Kathryn was in horrible pain. An acute anxiety arose within me, a biological fear of pain and annihilation, which felt unbearable. Why her and not me? I could feel her pain so acutely. I felt so guilty that I remained healthy while she was dying. I couldn't figure out how to live fully and plan for the future while both Kathryn and David were dying. My own life seemed to stall as each day I watched Kathryn make a heroic effort to just do the basic things in life.

Looking at her, you'd never have known she was sick; she had a slim figure, long, tan legs, aristocratic feet, and impeccably polished golden toes. Even on her worst days, she'd marshal her energy, put on her makeup, don an exquisite outfit with jewelry and shawl to match, and go out. I learned the high art of shopping from Kathryn: hunting for treasures that met her aesthetic standards at the lowest price! It didn't matter if we went to Ross, a thrift shop, or the toniest boutique, she quickly made a beeline for the most stylish items on the racks.

When we emptied her apartment after she died, we discovered many new items of clothing in her closet with tags still attached, bought for outings imagined but never experienced.

During this difficult time, she made two spiritual pilgrimages to India, visited a big-cat sanctuary, attended concerts, rested in a magnificent mountain sanctuary that had ocean views, and even hosted a final party to share an artsy, creative movie with her friends. Before she died, she had started a creative business that she called Adornments, selling hand-painted bandage stickers that could be applied over the ports that are inserted in the body for cancer treatment. She abhorred the ugly, and she loved making things beautiful.

She worked as a therapist up until the last three weeks of her life, saying that during those weeks, she did all of her best work. She knew time was short and had no superficial social filters to prevent her from saying what needed to be said.

We had endless discussions about the existential craziness of her situation: What's the point of it all? Is there a God? Where will I go after death? Is God beauty and love? She would say to me, "Do you think it's okay if I find God in the ocean at the beach? I talk to the Goddess as I walk on the beach; I give her a piece of my mind!"

I mostly remember laughing with her and finding the humor even in the most painful of situations. In the end, though, she couldn't beat her final challenge.

I missed the actual moment of her death; she died at the stroke of midnight, an hour after I went home to sleep. I drove back to her house in the early morning darkness and entered the hushed room where her body rested in peace on the bed, still warm but now just an empty shell. I took her hand and sobbed. Her soul seemed close, hovering over her body in unexpected freedom.

I watched her beautiful form, garlanded in flowers and dressed in white, decay and turn dark over the three days before she was taken for cremation. She had agreed before she died that she would send me a signal of some sort to let me know she was okay on the other side. No such signal came, so about a month later, I consulted a medium, John Cappello, who had no previous knowledge of her. After confirming her presence with precise details of her life, he relayed this message from Kathryn:

"Dani, I want you to understand that I now know that the Creator has a plan for us to perfect ourselves; that is the purpose of life. The moment of death is quite something—the angels come. For a while, I didn't know if I could let go of the pain, even though I didn't have a body. You will have your own moment, and when the time comes, I will be there for you."

I felt so comforted by these words.

One morning, shortly afterward, I felt her unmistakable presence during meditation. She arrived with our friend Alix, who had passed some years back. They giggled like fairy spirits as they sprinkled me with what felt like falling stardust, each particle embedded with light and wisdom. Then they blessed me through my crown and disappeared as quickly as they had arrived. I knew that this was her way of telling me that she was fine and was moving forward on the other side.

Rabbi Sandy

Rabbi Sandy died after a long struggle with an aggressive cancer that spread throughout her body. We had been in touch infrequently since I had moved to California.

Rabbi Sandy called me on a particularly difficult day during her treatment. She said, "I don't know if I will make it. I love you, and I treasure our friendship. I hope I can see you again. Are you coming back East?"

We cried together, and I promised to visit.

Just when things appeared most hopeless, she called again and jubilantly announced, "I've met someone."

"No kidding? Who?"

"Well, it's a woman; she's a doctor. She lost her partner to cancer a year or so ago. We've become very close."

Then a few months later, she called again and announced, "I have exciting news! We're getting married!"

I didn't know what to say. I couldn't believe that despite her grim prognosis, Rabbi Sandy had the courage to fall in love in the face of death. It blew me away that her doctor friend, despite her previous loss, had the courage to fall in love again with someone who was obviously not going to be around for very long. From Rabbi Sandy I learned that love is the ultimate container to hold opposites; only a heart tenderized by love can allow life and death to exist in such close proximity.

We never had closure. I saw her only once at the beginning of her illness. I was so completely absorbed in Kathryn's dying process that I couldn't face the loss of yet another dear friend.

Rabbi Sandy's spirited love of Judaism had finally conquered my resistance and allowed me to start the journey of return to my tradition. She left behind a wife, two daughters from her previous marriage, a mom, an ex-husband, and a diverse Jewish congregation in New Hope, Pennsylvania. I think of her whenever I attend Jewish services.

My Parents

When I arrived in Florida, I expected my dad to be at death's door; but despite his failing health, he seemed determined to live. He couldn't surrender. I sat by his side night after night, watching his breath, the constant beep of the oxygen machine marking the tempo of my nightly vigil. Sometimes his breath stopped, and I had to get very close to his chest to see if he was alive. Whenever my dad awoke, he, too, seemed surprised to find himself still in his body.

One night, he hardly breathed at all, and I lit a candle at his bedside. I jumped when he suddenly awoke and yelled at me: "Put that away! I don't want any of that!"

Although he didn't believe in an afterlife, one day he woke up from a nap and confided in me, "I just saw all my old buddies."

"What were they doing, Dad?"

"We were all at a bar, having a grand old time," he chuckled. "It was so good to see them!"

I guess the bar was the midway landing station for his soul as he practiced leaving his body. His dead buddies were waiting for him, drinks in hand.

My dad kept talking about a poem he remembered from high school: "Invictus," by William Ernest Henley. I looked it up on the Internet and read it to him. It brought tears to his eyes. It says more about his life than I could ever write.

> Out of the night that covers me,
> Black as the Pit from pole to pole,
> I thank whatever gods may be
> For my unconquerable soul.
> In the fell clutch of circumstance
> I have not winced nor cried aloud.
> Under the bludgeonings of chance
> My head is bloody, but unbowed.
>
> Beyond this place of wrath and tears
> Looms but the Horror of the shade,
> And yet the menace of the years
> Finds and shall find me unafraid.
>
> It matters not how strait the gate,
> How charged with punishments the scroll,
> I am the master of my fate,
> I am the captain of my soul.

For a while, my dad seemed to be perking up instead of dying. After three weeks of not eating, he was shouting for food. I made him scrambled eggs, which he ate with gusto.

I was exhausted and needed a break. I called my brother and asked him to come down to replace me so that I could go home to be with my friends, who had rented a sailboat and planned to spread Kathryn's ashes on the Pacific ocean.

I booked my flight, packed my bags, and went to say goodbye to my parents. For the first time in their sixty years together, they were sleeping in separate rooms. My dad lay on the couch in the den, attached to the oxygen machine. My mom lay unconscious on a hospital bed placed at the foot of their bed.

The onset of her Alzheimer's had revealed itself years ago when, at a restaurant, we all witnessed her order a meal; then, less than a minute later, ask for the waitress, not remembering that she had already ordered. My dad had probably hidden her behavior from us for some time, because he hadn't seemed shocked. Now, after eight years, Alzheimer's had stolen every bit of her ability to function. He had tried to care for her all by himself, refusing help until he could no longer cope.

The past week, she had been sick after contracting a virus that one of the aides had brought into the house, and she had now been unconscious for two days. I bent down over her frail body, engulfed in one of those cheap cotton nightgowns that button up the front so that her diapers could be easily changed.

I kissed her goodbye, brushing my cheek against her soft, dry skin.

"Bye, Mom. I'll be back. I love you," I said, as if she could hear me.

I thought I saw a flicker of a smile, a faint recognition in her expression.

I approached my dad, who barely nodded to me as I said goodbye.

"Thanks for everything, sweetie. Get home safe," he said. He didn't say, "I'll see you soon."

I returned to California in the late afternoon, immediately soothed by the beauty of Santa Barbara. Back in my cottage on the mountain, I fell into a deep sleep. At six thirty in the morning, the phone rang, and I stumbled to pick up the receiver, knowing the news would not be good.

My brother said: "I have bad news."

"Dad?" I asked.

"No, honey, Mom died this morning."

"Mom? I don't understand."

"Her breathing changed during the night. The aide and I sat by her side, and she stopped breathing at 3:30 a.m. She never regained consciousness."

"Oh, my God. I can't believe it. She went first! I know she did this for Dad. Is he okay? Did you tell him?"

"Yes, he knows. He turned his head away and closed his eyes when I told him."

"I'll book a flight."

"Don't rush back. You can stay there a day. You just got home. We can do the funeral in a few days. I will start to make the arrangements; they had it all planned, you know."

I hung up the phone in shock. I spent the rest of that day in a fog as we spread Kathryn's ashes from the boat, scattering them in the ocean near her favorite beach.

We had planned to move my mom to a memory care facility in Santa Barbara, if my dad went first. All that worry and planning, and nothing happened the way we had thought it would. My dad always said: "Don't worry, what will be will be. It will all work out." It turned out he was right.

On the plane ride back to Florida, images of the last difficult years of my mother's life floated through my mind: her obsessive ironing as she passed the iron over and over the same little square of cloth, watching her pour a whole bottle of honey in her tea, her pride in the childlike drawings that she did at the daycare facility, her delight in dancing—a skill that never left her, the day she smeared feces all over the walls of the daycare bathroom, her temper and frustration, her childlike sweetness, and her hair matted and white—so dramatically different from the perfectly coiffed black hairpiece she always wore.

What a contrast to the mom I had known before Alzheimer's decimated her mind: the mom who was the life of the party, the joke teller, the meticulous dresser, and the boss of the household. Her illness completely exhausted and exasperated my dad, but he remained by her side, steadfast and loyal in his love despite the constant stress. He wouldn't have done anything differently.

My dad died two days after my mother died. As soon as he knew she was taken care of, he finally surrendered. I know in my heart that my parents somehow planned this mystical departure. They were joined at the hip in life, so of course they would be together in death.

Two funerals—three days apart. Beyond surreal. The images of their fully dressed bodies lying in their coffins are imprinted in my memory—the last time I would ever see their mortal flesh. So eerie to sense their ghostly presences hovering over their own coffins. I wondered what they thought when seeing only twenty people in attendance; almost all their old friends were already gone.

It didn't matter that I knew there is life after death; that death is just a doorway and that consciousness goes on. Grief just piled up like a stack of heavy blankets atop my heart.

I felt like an orphan. I had no mother, no father. Death knocked the life out of me for a while. After three years of tending dying friends and parents, it took quite some time to gather my energy and recalibrate. Reality felt ephemeral. I existed in a liminal world stretched between the poles of life and death. My brain worked in slow motion.

All the urges to succeed and to promote myself dropped away. Just *being* felt more important than *doing*. I awoke in the mornings in a complete fog and couldn't get organized. I'd linger on the couch till some inner movement propelled me outside to walk. Every day, I walked for hours and then treated myself to matcha tea lattes, which I sipped slowly to avoid going to my office.

After all the estate sales, my own earthly possessions had little meaning as I imagined someone one day giving away all of my things: furniture, towels, dishes, photos, clothes—all no longer needed. Makes you think twice before buying more stuff.

My sister and I divided up my mom's jewelry. Now I wear her ring and bracelet, and every time I look down at my hand, I see her wrist and fingers overlaid upon mine.

I sometimes like to imagine my friend Kathryn finally reunited with her beloved cats: Missy, Tar Baby, Gipsy, Tom Tom, Wild Kitty, Beloved Tex, and Paco. I see her in a celestial art studio creating exquisite wearable objets d'art, which heal the people through a transmission of beauty.

And I envision Rabbi Sandy studying in a celestial academy with Kabbalistic sages who accept women as students.

David I see in a celestial laboratory, creating new ways to heal cancer with color, light, and holy speech.

And my parents . . . I picture them on the deck of the sailboat they never bought, practicing the cha-cha at sunset.

Sappy? Sure, but it works for me.

I joined the local IANDS group, the International Association of Near-Death Studies. Attending their monthly meetings gives me tremendous comfort. Listening to the reports of those who have crossed over and returned gives me the conviction, without a shadow of doubt, that there is life after death—or, as they would say, life after life.

People who have had near-death experiences report being in a wondrous world on the other side, where thought instantaneously creates reality. They report contact with an all-knowing, all-loving, indescribable Being of Light who communicates telepathically.

Not one of these near-death experiencers wants to return to their body, but they are told they have to come back because they still have something important to complete on the earth plane. They describe feeling loved way beyond a love they could ever dream of here in this realm—the love we all wish we had, a love they had known of all along but had somehow forgotten.

The universal message: Be impeccable now! Live your life fully! Don't waste time; it is a precious gift! Be kind!

We don't have to wait until we die to know such love; it is built into the very fabric of our universe. We just have to open our eyes to see it.

20

Celibacy

2002–present

The last thing a Vajra rising woman would ever want to be is celibate! Before I met Swamiji, I lived for the romantic highs and intensity of my encounters with men. I would never have imagined that I would end up being celibate. I also loved the companionship, sharing, cuddling, and the dance of intimacy in a long-term relationship and assumed I would one day remarry. My optimism about finding my "soul mate" remained intact despite my long list of disappointing relationships with men and the ensuing heartbreaks.

While being single is not anathema in our times, there is still much cultural pressure to be coupled. For most single women, myself included, we are trained early on to revolve our lives around the search for the partner: When am I going to meet "the one"? When am I going to get married?

I didn't even know whether I really wanted a partner, but I didn't want to hear that I *couldn't* have one. I often thought of the words of that tarot reader in Italy, the one who told me on my honeymoon: "You are not meant to be married in this life."

It has been hard to admit to myself that perhaps that message may be true.

So it is with some incredulity that, after fourteen years, I found myself quite content to be alone, without the compelling drive to be in relationship with a man. I never actually made a decision to be celibate; it seems that celibacy chose me.

In my early years with PKYC, every time I had an appointment to talk to Swamiji and Shivaji, I repeatedly asked, "When am I going to find a partner?"

Swamiji's answers changed gradually over time.

At first, he said: "See what God brings you."

I replied, "Okay . . . but God hasn't brought me anyone."

Some years later, Swamiji called me personally to thank me for referring a consultee to him in India. After a short conversation, he abruptly changed the topic, saying, "I can't tell you what to do, but it would be better if you stayed single and focused on your inner life. Man is a distraction for you. There were two Jewish sects: one was celibate and the other wasn't. It would be better if you were celibate."

I hung up the phone in shock. First, I was in shock that he had called me—not a common occurrence. Second, I was in shock at the message. Not what I had bargained for.

I think he had been referring to a small sect within the Essenes, a Jewish sect that lived at the time of Jesus and who practiced dietary restrictions and celibacy. This is unusual for Judaism, a tradition that strongly advocates marriage and family as the foundation for spiritual life. I had always felt as if I had been part of this sect in a past life, but I never quite understood what that had to do with me now in my current life.

Many people would say that Swamiji was just following the Advaita Vedanta monastic tradition, which tells us that our desires are distractions and will lead us astray.

However, just to be clear, celibacy is not generally recommended by PKYC; although they do recommend moderation and restraint in sexual activity so as to not deplete the prana system.

Also, Swamiji often encouraged people to find good marriage partners for the stability it gave to the person's physical life, saying, "How can you focus on your spiritual life if your physical and emotional life isn't stable? In India, marriages were arranged so that the young couple cultivated their intention toward the Divine at a very early age. They were instructed in how to focus their attention so that when the marriage was consummated, they improved their Kundalini process."

Similarly, the Jewish tradition holds marriage as the sacred container for a divinely led life, and the act of intercourse is viewed as a holy interaction. In the Talmud (primary Jewish text), there are numerous detailed instructions as to the appropriate timing, frequency, and intent during the act of intercourse.

I didn't push the issue. I decided to just see what happened. I noticed that as Kundalini cleared and repaired my chakras and subtle body, I had less and less of a longing to find the beloved outside myself. Meditation became an effortless resting within a deeply embodied velvety silence and produced a deep contentment that sourced from within that which I sought outside myself.

Eight or nine years of being alone had gone by when I again brought up the question of a relationship in my session with Swamiji and Shivaji.

I whined, "Why can't I have a partner? Lots of your other consultees, including those with Vajra risings, have partners."

Shivaji responded, "Even in a loving and committed relationship, the sexual aspect has its own kind of energy that is heavier. It is such a deep drive for everyone. For you, in particular, as a Vajra rising woman, with your history of romantic yearning and sexual trauma, the man is a distraction, even though it may be what you want the most.

"If you were partnered, you would not go to the depth of your spiritual life or to the depth of the spiritual work which is to come, if you had a husband and children. Your calling is to be the person who gives some assistance to the ones who want to become advanced spiritual practitioners. If you had a husband, lover, or grandchildren, you would just become absorbed in them. It would distract you from this ascetic calling, which you actually do have, perhaps against your personality's will. What you are being asked to do is hold the living container, the larger vessel of your tradition. Sex is a compelling drive for everyone. For you it's an obsession."

Her words rang true. I said, "I know. I always give myself away to the man; I know I get completely obsessed. I lose myself, and then I try to become what he wants me to be."

Shivaji commented, "If Swamiji had said 'no men' to you on your first retreat, you would have fled."

How true.

Although Swamiji had been an ordained monk for more than fifty years, he surprised us all when he told us about his past situation before he met his own master:

"I was a very bad, sexy, Vajra rising man in this life. I had very bad damage to my subtle body through sex. I blamed myself."

Wow, I thought, Swamiji himself had a Vajra rising! He, too, had to overcome this amplified desire for sex!

Swamiji continued, "When I first met my master, he rejected me and said that I was not fit to study yoga. I went away, but that wasn't good for me. I went back to my master and asked him again to teach me."

"My master said, 'First I will teach you to cook. Food is important for the body, and right food will fix your problems.'

"So I learned how to cook. Eventually, my subtle body was in good enough condition for Kundalini to be diverted into *Chitirini* nadi in the central column. Later, my master told me to get married. But I said, 'No, I will take *sannyas* and be a monk.'"

Later in his life, when he was a wandering monk, Swamiji ministered to women with female problems using Ayurvedic medicine. In this way, he repaired his own karmic relationship with women and became an expert on the problems of the female hormonal system and the different ways that unhealthy sexual relationships can damage the subtle body.

I once asked him how he found the strength to keep his monastic vows.

He looked directly into my eyes and said softly, "It is very hard. The sexual energy doesn't go away; it is the life force! The experience of orgasm is the greatest opportunity for human beings to have a glimpse of the experience of pure consciousness. For that one moment, all five senses are involved, and simultaneously the mind stills. You catch the gap between thoughts, and you taste the Oneness. But this experience doesn't last.

"If you get addicted to the action of sex, and you mis-use it, it causes damage in the subtle body, and you don't get enlightenment. Without a good movement of energy to the second chakra, you can't have a healthy aura. The second chakra is connected with the entire hormone system. When sexual energy is abused, it affects the part of the brain that produces neurotransmitters and endor-phins. When they are depleted, it causes addiction.

"If the sexual experience makes you yearn for lasting liberation, it's good. Only liberation can give you the real experience of Oneness, the One without a second."

My own addiction to sex played out in the dream state for many years. I had extremely vivid sexual dreams with men that I seemed to know quite well. I reported some of the dreams to Swamiji. He explained that Kund-alini was clearing my past lives and not to give too much attention to the dreams.

I practiced writing down the dreams and observing them as a film of my past, running through the projec-tor so that it could be dissolved. But, boy, some of those dreams were technicolor vivid, accompanied by full sen-sory memory, and I would wake up panting and on the verge of orgasm, only to realize it was just a dream. Real but not real . . .

Swamiji explained, "When the mind can't go outside and use sensory objects for pleasure, then it remembers those objects in dreams. In the dream, the dreamer feels the dream is real. All dream experience is from the past. Our present life is a product of our past lives. Our current temptations and distractions are based on our past sams-karas and vasanas. The science of yoga teaches us that to get over these tendencies, we have to have profound obser-vation of our thoughts with dispassion and discrimination."

Getting Tested

A few weeks before I left for Florida to be with my dying parents, at a time in my life when I felt stressed out and vulnerable, a man came into my life. I thought he would be a friend for life, not a potential romantic partner. Nev-ertheless, just being near him stimulated my long-lost craving for sex and intimacy. After eleven years of celi-bacy, my pattern of obsessing over "the man" came back in full force!

While I was in Florida, we communicated every day, giving me a rush of endorphin support to get through this difficult time. A casual intimacy quickly grew between us, based on our constant exchange of clever and funny text messages. In fact, he inspired me to craft the most amusing text messages I have ever written. I began to rely on him for emotional support.

He said, "I am here for you as your parents are dying. You can call me anytime, day or night." And I did.

I knew when he was thinking of me because I felt waves of sexual desire flood my body, despite the great distance between us. It felt similar to how I felt when Sananda visited me astrally at night. Much later, Shivaji told me that it is possible that this man had a form of Vajra "sex magic" that he could use for seduction. He could extend a part of his energy body outward from his sexual center using Vyana vayu, the energetic movement of the second chakra, and could actually touch someone sexually with it.

Like a trained mouse, at the sound of a text coming through, my heart would race, and the endorphins related to connection would flood my being. I knew I was in trouble when I started keeping my cell phone by my meditation cushion so that I could answer his texts during my practice!

Swayed by the activity in my second chakra, I wrote Swamiji and Shivaji, describing him and saying, "I think I may be ready for a relationship again. Perhaps he is a timely gift from the Divine Mother?"

I immediately received a time for a phone appointment.

As soon as Swamiji picked up the phone, his "silver hammer" once again came down upon my head, slamming my hope that this man could be my partner.

He said with fierce intensity, "You don't need a man to be happy. This relationship won't work out for you. For a Vajra woman like you, the man is a distraction. You will lose all your concentration. Make your feelings concentrate on God, not man. You came to me many years ago, saying that you keep making the same mistakes. If you go back to men now, it will take three more lifetimes to reach the level you are at now, and I won't be here to help you! Be strong. Have self-responsibility, dispassion, and self-discipline!"

I froze, like the proverbial deer in the headlights, and I barely remember anything else he said. Shivaji barely got a word in.

Swamiji scolded, "If you go back to the left path and get stuck in the belief that sexuality equals God, you will be lost in the River of Fire and never get out of it.

"No man!!!" he yelled at me.

I still didn't quite believe him, but the River of Fire didn't sound too welcoming.

After I hung up the phone, my heart cracked open in grief. Torrents of heartrending tears had me clenching my stomach, doubled over in pain. This pain seemed to be so much larger than the current situation. I couldn't stop crying.

Why should I listen to him? This isn't normal. Nothing is excluded from the Divine, including relationships. This doesn't make any sense. He is just trying to put fear into me.

Then my thoughts went in the opposite direction: Swamiji has been the most amazing mentor, teacher, and spiritual guide I have ever met. He has always been in integrity and has no personal agendas with his students. What would happen if he *is* right this time around? I have had many lifetimes being married, having kids, but I have not devoted a life to spiritual realization or had the right help before now. What if he's right?

In the morning, still unable to stop crying, I called Shivaji. "I don't know what's happening. . . . I can't stop crying. I have never felt grief like this," I choked out between sobs.

She soothed me, like a mother would console a child, and just listened as I sobbed.

"You have hit one of those 'hidden boulders' in your psyche," she said. "This man has brought it forth. It is a samskara that could only appear after the other layers had been cleared. As a Vajra rising woman, you probably had previous Tantric training, and you came into this life with a strong belief that you could get enlightened through sex. This is simply not true, no matter what modern-day

Tantra teaches, unless the practitioner knows the secret esoteric method to enable a diversion of Kundalini into a culminating nadi. Eventually, the lover and the beloved must dissolve into the One in the Brahma nadi at Bindu."

I kept up the contact with this man until my parents died. I was too needy, too devastated by the thought of losing my parents, to cut him off. I needed to have a confidant. Although my other friends checked in often, he provided a steady stream of support.

Then, right after my parents died, something shifted. His humor and kindness disappeared. His texts became less frequent. As soon as I got home from Florida, he abruptly withdrew as if we had never known each other. He became too busy to see me and didn't return my messages.

I found out later that he was on to the next conquest. I also realized how much I had been in a trance. I got to see his real lack of character and integrity rather quickly once I was home. Yet his withdrawal just added fuel to the fire of my grief. I realized that his wanting to be of service to me had more to do with enhancing his self-image as a savior and less to do with being a true friend.

At that time, being a human being felt unbearable.

In the mornings, I took long walks along the mountain ridge, and when I went uphill, anger and grief would rise upward through my heart and erupt in heaving sobs. And then an inner switch flipped, and waves and waves of bliss began to wash through me, flooding the innermost crannies of my soul with joy. It felt like a wild roller coaster that catapulted me over the highest peaks and down into the lowest valleys. How could these two states oscillate so quickly?

Even though I was practiced at holding opposites from my work as a Kabbalistic healer, it required a lot of stamina and resiliency to hold these extremes of emotion. I prayed to the Divine Mother to give me the capacity to bear witness to these oscillating states as she tenderized and stretched my heart to its capacity. How hard it is to be with all of reality—just as it is.

From where I sit now, celibacy has become a nonissue. It impressed me that Swamiji disagreed with his own teacher and became a monk against his advice. I gave myself permission to disagree with Swamiji on the whole issue of celibacy. However, nothing changed. I found to my surprise that I was content in my life and didn't desire any change. For me, celibacy is not a rejection of partnership; it just emerged gradually as the way of life that most suited me.

I treasure my solitude. I am not isolated, and I have a large group of friends with whom I am regularly in contact. There are three men in my life that have been the dearest of friends for years. They are "soul mates" in the deepest sense of the word. Yet I still can't say I have taken a vow of celibacy, nor can I know what is next. I prefer to just see what life brings me.

21

Completion

Knoxville, Tennessee, June 2013

*The Eternal One is God in the heavens above and on the
earth below; there is nothing else.*

   —the Aleynu (the prayer concluding a Jewish service)

Two months after my parents died, I felt exhausted
from the cumulative impact of all the losses in my life. I
couldn't get motivated to do anything, plan anything, or
be anything.

The immediate stressors were gone, but when I
awoke in the mornings, my nervous system immediately
activated the hyperalert switch, as if I were still waiting
for "the call" that would inform me of my parents' deaths.
The reality that they had passed seeped in slowly.

I booked a retreat in Knoxville with Swamiji and
Shivaji to recalibrate and restore my energy. I arrived
in the late afternoon and felt so comforted to be in the
familiar basement setting of Shivaji's home. The familiar
vibration of sanctity and peace soothed me. I unpacked
my bags and curled up on my bed until dinner.

I met my fellow retreatants over our evening meal: the usual soup, veggies, and toast. I felt like a wise old-timer, as this was my eighth retreat. I had requested the smallest room without windows because it felt like a cave and a healing chamber. I retired early and slept deeply.

In the morning, after breakfast and practice, Swamiji and Shivaji called me upstairs to Shivaji's sunny office. I sat down opposite Swamiji in a comfortable armchair. He looked at me with great kindness and immediately began to speak.

"Now your life is different; your parents have passed and you are alone. Death is not the end; it is the changing of the old cloth with the new one. Everything is the will of God. The body is perishable, but the subtle body continues. For the first time, you are secure. You have lived a long time insecure, and you suppressed upset feelings. Now you can keep your feelings positive and bring very strong focus toward God."

"Swamiji," I said, "I have had a lot of brain fog. I feel depressed, and even though I am on hormones, my hair is falling out."

"If you eat a little meat, you will get some testosterone; eat a little chicken and lamb. Even some fish will make you feel better and improve your muscle tone."

"Meat?" I asked, thinking I hadn't heard right. Although I always ate some fish and eggs, I hadn't eaten animal meat in over twenty years.

Shivaji said, "Even I am eating some chicken these days. Long-term vegetarians can get physically depleted. Westerners who were not brought up vegetarian and have no DNA ancestry of vegetarianism can have trouble sustaining vegetarianism without getting sick or losing muscle tone."

Swamiji continued, "You have been very distracted, and your process got stuck again. One has to have discrimination to become free from illusion, and anyone can slip, even after they surpass Bindu.

"For you, the draw toward sex is so compelling. When you come near a man, your system takes the vibration of his testosterone. It makes you happy because it produces oxytocin. But this vibration makes you go unconscious. You have to develop dispassion and say to yourself: *I am happy, I have everything I need inside of me. The world can't make me happy.*"

"I understand, Swamiji."

I really did get it. It became so clear to me just how distracted I get when my attention is focused on a man. The man becomes the All. When centering on my practice, my heart opened even more, and I began to feel anchored in a greater love, one not based on attachment and possessiveness.

"We will give you your new practices tomorrow," he said. The interview ended and I went downstairs.

The days settled into the usual schedule: morning practice, breakfast, rest, late-morning practice, lunch, rest, late-afternoon practice, dinner, rest, late-evening practice, sleep. My whole being craved the discipline and structure. I received my new practices, and within a few days, I felt revitalized, and my mind became quiet and peaceful.

One night, my sleep felt different. Awareness was present during the deep sleep state. I thought: Oh, this is what the yogis mean when they say they are awake within the sleep state. I rested in "sleep" while awake without tossing or turning, and I didn't feel at all tired the next day.

Around seven a.m., I went outside to have a cup of tea on the patio before the morning practice. The birds sang in a harmonious symphony of tones as they flitted to and from the numerous bird feeders hanging from the deck above. The air was humid and moist, and the temperature was already climbing. I sat, sipped my tea, senses wide open, content, just being in the moment and not thinking about anything at all.

I watched the movement of a tiny ant near my feet, carrying a piece of a leaf at least four times its body size. It walked around in circles carrying this oversized parcel in its mouth.

In that moment, suddenly my mind went completely clear and vast. It became as vast as eternity itself.

No thought, no person, no history, no physicality, no time.

A few seconds or minutes may have passed. My sense of "I-ness" disappeared into Awareness itself.

When my mind returned, I heard a voice that said: "The ant is like us, walking around in circles with our load of *Chitta*, our conditioned mind stuff. We can put this burden down at any time if we want to and be lighter and clearer. This is what the mind feels like when it doesn't make stories, when it is not weighed down by the past."

I walked inside to do my morning practice. One part of my practice involved contemplating the nondual nature of God through repeating the phrase, "Everything and Nothing. Nothing and Everything."

As soon as I started the repetition, the words "Everything and Nothing" and "Nothing and Everything" became One. They collapsed into each other, and "I" dissolved into light. All that remained present was a sense of awareness within the One Absolute Reality. It also seemed to me that the Tree of Life within me folded upward into the Oneness, it, too, dissolving into the light. "I" remained in undifferentiated Oneness for some time.

From then on, "I" knew with certainty that there is only One Absolute Reality, and all the nondual teachings became real.

Everything changed in that moment, and nothing changed.

I eventually got up, ate breakfast, and life continued just as before. However, my perception of life, God, and the spiritual path was forever altered.

All questing for "enlightenment" ceased then and there. Questing for what? How can one quest for the all-pervading Vastness that has no form yet is what underlies all form; the Vastness that cannot be known with the mind; that is not a thing to be achieved or acquired yet is both everything and nothing. A nothing that is filled with something unnameable, yet also knowable through consciousness. This is the One without a second, pure awareness without name, form, opposites, or attributes.

I had a good laugh about the irony of a little ant showing me the true nature of reality, as my last name is "Antman." I had always joked with friends that when I realized *Atman*, the true self of the individual, beyond identification with phenomena, I would lose the first "n" in my last name. The Great Intelligence does seem to have a sense of humor.

It became interesting to observe without judgment the different levels of human experience that moved through me. Grief, for example, continued in rollercoaster waves. Grief is our biologically wired response to loss of a person to whom we feel attached. Yet this same vast awareness was present in grief, just as it is present in anger, joy, bliss, and every other human experience. Or perhaps it is more accurate to say these experiences are present within the Vastness.

When I have a human reaction that I am not proud of, I can cognitively trace it back to its source without separating out of this awareness. Even when I do "lose" this awareness and feel separate, the awareness is still aware, watching itself feel divided from itself. Hard to explain, it is what I had always read about but never actually realized: how the experience of wholeness/awareness includes and is not separate from the illusion of separation and the play of all the opposites. Everything that arises is made of the "nothingness that is everything." Universes, people, objects, the smallest forms of matter to the largest planets in the solar system—all animated by this same unconditioned awareness.

My twelve years of intense Kundalini process finally came to completion. Strange that everything remained the same. Afterward, everything felt ordinary. I didn't become a saint or any concept of an enlightened person that I had previously envisioned. I also knew that my spiritual growth hadn't ended; there needed to be more stabilization and integration of this awareness. I still had a very human personality but truly didn't reject it as something that was separate from this awareness.

Everything is included within the all-encompassing Vastness. I have never looked at reality the same way again. It was as if the curtain in the *Wizard of Oz* had been drawn back, and instead of seeing the wizard, I saw Reality itself.

About a week after I went home, I pulled into my driveway and was about to get out of the car to take my groceries into the house. Again, I became absorbed in the Vastness, and my perception of the world disappeared. It was as if the underlying background of Vastness became the foreground, and the world vanished into the background. Or another way of putting it is that the veils that hid the Vastness dropped away. I understood in that moment that the veils serve a purpose; for if a person were unprepared for this experience, it could be terrifying. It lasted for what may have been seconds or minutes; I don't know, because there was no "I" present having an experience.

Then the world returned, and I simply got out of the car and took the groceries inside.

22

Liberation Is at Hand

Knoxville, Tennessee, June/July 2014

I am the all. I am the All in all. I am the One in all. I am
the all in One. I am the many.

—Brahmanubhava Upanishad

After my 2013 retreat, Swamiji announced that he would
no longer be present at our practice retreats. He also
announced that he would offer six more Self-Illumination
Therapy Training Intensives (SITTI) the following summer and that, after that, he would no longer be coming
back to the United States. He was approaching eighty-
five and was ready to hand over the American PKYC to
Shivaji.

Swamiji gave an overview of all his teachings over
the course of the six SITTI intensives, using the texts that
he had studied his whole life that informed the methods
he used: Kundalini Vidya, the Yoga Sutras, Tattva Bodha,
Laghu Vakya Vrtti, and the Upanishads. I attended the
last two of these six intensives in June and July 2014.

We gathered in a three-car garage that Shivaji
had converted into a classroom, outfitted with air

conditioning, cushy swivel seats, and small desks for about thirty people. Every morning, we chanted the Shanti Mantras, prayers that begin the Upanishads. This created an intensely charged atmosphere by the time Swamiji entered at ten a.m.

Each morning, Swamiji looked around the room, apparently scanning our brains to determine our state of mind. He declared solemnly, "These will be 'silver hammer' intensives!"

And, indeed, they were: every word he uttered seemed to pound a transmission of the knowledge from the texts into my poor brain. After three hours of class in the morning and three more in the afternoon, my brain was fried.

His main message was that even though most of us were in Upper process, we couldn't smugly rest there if we wanted final liberation.

Swamiji said, "Liberation is at hand, but the ball is in your court! I keep the ball in your court, not my court. If you are strong, you can play with me for win-win. Or you can be the runner-up."

He scolded us, "Unless you apply rigorous self-effort for the rest of your lives, you will be like a hamster in a cage, just spinning the wheel. You can stay stuck in Upper process, and you won't make any progress."

I knew then, by his intense desire to give us teachings that we could utilize for the rest of our lives, that I would not see him again in physical form. It made every moment precious, and he didn't mince words. He pounded into us the message that we couldn't be lazy in our spiritual practice and rest on our laurels.

He said, "I can't fulfill your high expectations without you filling your responsibilities! You are the one responsible for erasing the samskaras and vasanas. No one can do that for you; you have to do it yourself. Even swamis can fall into the valley of distraction. Even if you have the highest experience, the atom bomb of samskaras and vasanas can still get you.

"You need self-confidence, self-effort, and willpower. Distraction is a very big issue. Everyone is very active making a living. You seem successful, but you harm yourself. Don't deplete the vitality of your prana. Keep your prana level high! High! High! Prana is the visible Brahman. It is the great gift for the human brain. It makes birth and death and works in the chakra system so that we can attain liberation."

The Four-Inch Gap

Swamiji asked rhetorically, "How do we not allow duality and all the polarities to take over our lives? How do we keep the focus on Oneness while still living in duality?"

He then explained, "If you make the mind have one thought, you catch the gap between thoughts. There is a four-inch gap between the individual personal consciousness and the universal Absolute Consciousness. You can't see it; it is a metaphor for that which creates our sense of separation and duality.

"When the mind has one thought, through one pointed concentration in meditation, that gap closes, and you experience Absolute Consciousness. Self-illumination illuminates the gap, and the mind stops making stories. At the moment of orgasm, this happens, too, which is why you experience bliss, union, and a moment of no self at that time. However, the orgasm is just a glimpse experience. Dedicated meditation practice closes this gap."

With chagrin, I realized that even though I'd had the nonreversible, culminating realization that the world and the Self are One Absolute Reality, it was not yet a permanent view; and even though the experience still feels as real as concrete for me, I still commute between the phenomenal world and the One. However, there is an expanding experience of Oneness that pervades daily life.

When I meditate, I am quickly absorbed in Unitive consciousness. There is no "I" doing a practice. There is no experience to talk about. When absorption stops of its own accord, the phenomenal world returns. The next stage of meditation is seeing the world, the universe, the manifest, and the unmanifest as One all the time.

I thought back to the Healing of Immanence, the Kabbalistic healing I had learned at ASOS that is predicated on receiving the immanent divinity of the person and their presenting complaint or illness. I realized it was a good practice, a valid starting point that eventually could culminate in the embodied realization of this truth. However, it does not happen without the corresponding inner work and subtle-body preparation that needs to be there for permanent nondual realization.

Swamiji said, "There are seven different steps of *samadhi* [absorption] after Kundalini Shakti has reached Bindu at the top of the head."

He quoted a translation of a Vedic text called *Drg Drysa Viveka*:

> "In Nirvikalpa samadhi, the mind becomes steady and not identified with anything. It stays in its own nature, Oneness. There is no second. But even in Nirvikalpa samadhi, there are two kinds: inferior and superior. Inferior is when you are inside; superior is

when the inner experience is in the outer also. Then it is superior Nirvikalpa samadhi. It is only then that the three knots of illusion are dissolved (heart, desire, and karma) and then all doubts disappear. Then one is beyond grief, beyond fear, beyond death, immortal."

His explanation illuminated quite clearly why one continues to meditate and what happens as levels of absorption (samadhi) deepen, until the outer and the inner are the same.

Swamiji never presented his work as transcendence over "matter." Our practices worked *through* our physical bodies and subtle bodies. He emphasized the importance of good-quality food, a peaceful, supportive environment and setting up our lives so that they were conducive to consistent spiritual practice.

In yogic language, one eventually becomes a *Jivanmukta*, someone who is fully awake on all levels in all worlds and is liberated while still in a body. A Jivanmukta is awake in the waking, dreaming, and deep-sleep states and has achieved *Turiyatita*, the condition of always being one with the One, and is freed from the cycles of birth and death.

In the Jewish tradition, after one has realized the *Ain*, the nothingness that is everything, there is also a return to the physical world with the recognition that the world and all its duality are *one*, which is very similar to the Jivanmukta of the Vedic path.

Swamiji's self-realized presence validated for me that, yes, there is a final liberation from the world of form, dependent upon the completion of all of one's karmas and the clearing of all the vasanas and samskaras. This is no small task and could possibly take many lifetimes after one has reached Makara. Yet even Swamiji had to live out his *prarabdha* karma, the karma that cannot be changed and that must be completed by the person while they are in a body. The prarabdha karma is nonnegotiable.

The Jivanmukta truly sees everything and everyone as that Absolute Oneness. It is still a very rare and advanced state. Before one has attained this state, practice is still necessary. After one has attained this state, practice seems unnecessary, for why would you need to practice being what you already are by your very nature. Nonetheless, "practice" continues; it arises naturally.

This creates a lot of confusion in the way nonduality is taught in the West, which makes it seem as if spiritual practice is not effective or necessary. The existence of unpurified, deeply held vasanas and samskaras, in even the most advanced spiritual practitioners, accounts for much of the "shadow" behavior exhibited by proclaimed enlightened teachers. According to Swamiji, without consistent practice, they will not be cleared and the experience of Oneness will not stabilize.

I had to leave the retreat a few days early due to some prior commitments, and I had my final personal interview with Swamiji. There wasn't a lot said; he reiterated his admonitions from the intensive. What I mostly received was his love, and what I expressed to him was my eternal gratitude. I went home filled with peace and grace, not needing anything. I felt complete within my Self.

Swamiji's Passing

Over the next two years, Swamiji had some health concerns with his heart. He recovered and hinted that he would be around for a while. He was training an Austrian woman named Silvia Eberl to take over his work in India.

In February 2016, Shivaji received a call from a radiantly happy Swamiji, who asked her, "Are you sure you have everything you need to carry on in life?"

She said, "Yes, Swamiji."

"Health is okay?"

"Yes, Swamiji."

"I am finished with my karmas," he announced jubilantly.

Little did she realize at the time how quickly he would leave his body.

Swamiji was not the type to prepare everyone for the day of his final departure. He didn't like fuss or undue attachment.

On March 15, he had a heart attack. He remained unconscious and noncommunicative for the next two weeks, then left his body for good on March 30, 2016. He had just turned eighty-six.

At noon on March 30 in the United States (a day later than in India), I was driving to meet two friends for lunch. I heard the voicemail beep on my phone, and I glanced down and saw a message from Shivaji.

I pulled over to the side of the road with a sense of foreboding and played her voicemail message.

"Dani, it's Shivaji. I wanted to tell you in person: Swamiji left his body yesterday at five thirty in the evening EST. The monks who knew him for thirty years prepared his body to be submerged in the holy river Ganges, as he wished, so he is free now. I sent you an email explaining things. I love you; don't grieve, be happy for him."

Pain pierced my heart at the news of his death, and I burst into tears. Somehow, I made it to the restaurant, where I sat outside until my friends arrived. They saw me crying and came to sit beside me.

"I just found out my spiritual teacher has died," I choked out. I heaved with sobs, despite Shivaji's admonition to not grieve. They each took one of my hands and sat with me till I could talk again. I told them about Swamiji and how much he meant to me.

Gradually, I calmed down enough to go inside for lunch, but my head still swam with the news of this enormous loss. I couldn't imagine Swamiji being gone and my no longer having the benefit of his spiritual guidance. Although I hadn't spoken to him often during the past two years, just knowing that his wisdom and advice were available gave me great spiritual comfort. It was yet another loss in my series of losses over the last few years.

Over lunch, the texts started pouring in from my friends and fellow consultees, expressing their shock over the news. I felt a strong urge to go back to India to have closure.

Later, I read Shivaji's email explaining that there would be a *bandhara*, a feast prepared for three hundred sadhus (renunciates), in Rishikesh in Swamiji's honor. According to tradition, a bandhara is offered sixteen days after a great being's passing, and Shivaji said that if we felt moved to come to India, we would be welcome to attend the feast.

Shivaji informed us that Swamiji had already had a *jal* (water) burial in the Ganges. Swamiji had requested this special type of burial rather than being interred with the other lineage holders who had passed on, who were enshrined in the sacred temple compound of Kaleshwar, the founding place of his lineage.

She wrote, "Within twenty-four hours, fellow monks who knew him and loved him had washed and garlanded his body, anointed it with ash, and built a special crate with slatted sides, with which to put him in the water. They placed him on a palanquin, processed him through town and carried him to the Ganges river. There, on the banks of the river, they lovingly put him in the crate, weighed it down with river rocks, and pushed him into the river that he regarded as the body of the Divine Goddess herself."

I quickly searched for my passport, only to find that it had expired two years ago. By the time I decided I definitely wanted to go to India for the feast, I had less than a week to get a passport and visa. I took a day off from work to go to Los Angeles to get my passport renewed, and I managed to obtain a thirty-day visa online. I paid expediting fees for everything, and the travel plans took hours to make, but finally all my affairs were in order and I was ready to go.

Saturday, the day of my upcoming evening flight, I attempted to check in online, and to my utter shock received an automatic message saying that I could not check in for my flight because it was already in the air! I had missed my flight. I had mistaken the time of departure for the evening when it had actually been in the morning. With yet another flurry of calls and fees, I rebooked a flight for the next day.

I had a long but uneventful trip from LAX to Newark airport, where I joined a female consultee from Michigan for the thirteen-and-a-half-hour flight to New Delhi. If I hadn't missed my flight, we would not have traveled together. We arrived in New Delhi at nine thirty p.m. local time and took a cab to the Holiday Inn at the airport for a night's sleep.

In the morning, we met up with another consultee, a woman who has been a long-time colleague of mine.

Together, the three of us hired a driver and embarked on the six-hour drive to Rishikesh. The constant swerving of the car as it nearly collided with cows, carts, and oncoming traffic made me nauseous and sleepy. When we stopped for lunch in an Indian restaurant, I felt grateful to sit still, even for a short time. Three hours later, we finally arrived at our hotel, right near Swamiji's apartment in Rishikesh.

After the porter took my bags to my room, I quickly headed back out. I joined four other American consultees to pay our respects at the spot on the Ganges river where Swamiji's body had been submerged.

We took a gasoline-powered rickshaw, winding through the noisy, crowded streets of Rishikesh to a street corner that led to the river. We purchased some handmade leaf bowls, filled with marigolds, incense, and a bit of camphor to light, as an offering in Swamiji's honor.

I carried my bowl down to the river and sat with my bare feet dangling in the cool, frothy, greenish current that tumbled down from the Himalayas. I cried softly as I imagined my beloved Swamiji's body right below the surface. I offered silent prayers in gratitude to Swamiji, and I immediately felt blasted by an intense illumination from above. Clearly, it was a response from Swamiji, who seemed to be even more present and available than when he was in a body.

A sadhu with a wiry, grey beard, who looked like he had been squatting along the riverbanks for eons, insisted on helping us light and launch our flower-leaf boats. His help was more of a hindrance, diverting my focus from Swamiji's radiant presence. The daylight began to fade, and we left just as the lights on the distant suspension bridge that crossed the river began to twinkle in the background.

On the way back, we bought garlands of flowers, then went to Swamiji's apartment to see Shivaji, who had arrived a few days earlier. Shivaji, Silvia, and around ten other visitors sat around the dinner table. The room looked the same as it had when I had last visited seven years earlier. How precious that time with him seemed right now.

The electrical charge that is the signature of Swamiji's elevated presence was even more pronounced in his absence, and it sanctified the spare décor—a few bookcases and posters on the otherwise bare walls.

The dining room table had been expanded to make room for the guests. Swamiji's empty chair seemed to await his return, as if he had just gotten up from the table. Only the flowers draped over its back indicated that wasn't so.

I greeted everyone and gently placed my garland of marigolds at the base of a large picture—Swamiji in samadhi—sitting on a low table set up as an altar.

I joined the group seated at the table, who were already engaged in a project for the bandhara. We each received a pile of beautiful gold-embossed envelopes to fill with a one-hundred-rupee bill. We then affixed a small, round, gold Om label on the front and sealed the back with a small piece of tape. These would be part of the gifts offered to the sadhus the next day. Our job complete, we retired for the evening.

I and two others were the first to arrive at the Kartikeya Temple a few miles up the road from our hotel. The temple's rainbow-colored spires, covered with figures from the Indian pantheon of gods, made it easily identifiable from the street. Inside, the head swami welcomed us and quickly pulled out some chairs for us.

The monks hurried about as they prepared the court-yard for the feast. They unrolled one-foot-wide burlap strips, which seemed to have more dirt in them than the dirt on the floor, to form four "carpets" for the sadhus to sit upon. The courtyard must have been at least one hundred feet long, and overhead a purple-and-white-patterned Indian fabric shielded the area from the harsh sun.

As the others arrived, I walked around and observed the huge vats of rice and dal being prepared outside. One sadhu rolled dough for puris (fried bread), and I watched as he dropped each ball into the hot oil and it puffed up into light, flying-saucer-shaped bread.

The swami ushered us toward the temple to the left of the courtyard, where we could sit and pray. We walked up hand-decorated marble steps to approach the entrance. There, upon a covered table, was a draped and garlanded photo of Swamiji with offerings of fruit and flowers before it. As I knelt in front of it, tears welled up in my eyes. The truth of his passing sunk in.

Soon the sadhus, who had been invited by the heads of several local ashrams, began filing in. Some were teen-agers, others very old men, and they all wore the monas-tic orange cloth, though the shades of orange varied from saffron yellow to deep burnt orange. One very tall sadhu wore a pink cloth! Their etched faces would have made a compelling cover for *National Geographic* magazine. A few women sadhus sat amongst them and regarded us Ameri-can women with twinkling eyes.

The whole place buzzed with a high vibration as the head swamis led a chant in Swamiji's honor, ending with a victory cheer.

As the food was served, we paired up and distributed the gifts to the sadhus in honor of Swamiji's passing: a new *dhoti* (saffron cloth), an envelope with some rupees, a flashlight, a *mala* (a string of 108 *rudrashka* prayer beads), and a pair of rubber flip-flops.

As I went down the rows, passing out the flip-flops, I was amused that the sadhus called out their shoe size in an attempt to get the right fit.

After three rounds of sadhus had eaten and received gifts, we were invited to sit down and eat. I discreetly avoided eating, as my digestion is delicate and I didn't want to risk getting sick. The feast ended, the last of the monks filed out, and the burlap carpets were rolled up and put away.

For the rest of the week in Rishikesh, I took day trips with two friends to visit sacred sites: the sage Vashista's cave, the shrine of the bliss-intoxicated Indian saint Anandamayi Ma, and a place two hours north of Rishikesh called Devprayag, the point at which the Alaknanda and Bhagirathi rivers merge and take the name Ganges. Hanuman is said to have left his footprints on a boulder at this very spot.

We submerged our bodies, fully clothed, into the sacred river and received her blessings. After we had immersed ourselves in the frothy green currents, a sadhu approached us and, while chanting blessings, applied *kumkuma* powder at our Ajna chakras between the eyebrows.

I felt cleansed and renewed, ready to start the long journey home.

I traveled back to New Delhi without my two friends, in a hired car. The acrid air pollution in the city choked me, so after a little shopping, I spent a day and a night in my hotel room so as not to breathe the air. I flew out in the evening and arrived home after the impossibly long flights, exhausted but filled with gratitude.

Since Swamiji's death, he has been viscerally present as an impersonal light; a bright consciousness above, beyond, and within my head; a consciousness that I sense is helping me when I do my practice.

Afterword

Santa Barbara, 2016

*Then again, what is wanted is a genuine Awakening, an
awakening after which nothing remains to be obtained. . . .
To be fully conscious is not enough, you will have to rise
beyond consciousness and unconsciousness. That Which
Is has to shine forth.*

—Anandamayi Ma

The great Cosmic Joke is that we come into the world
with an illusion of separation so that each of us can go on
a journey to the source of what we already are! By grace,
we are given the very vehicle that is perfect for us to complete the journey, the gift of our human life.

I have come full circle, having discovered a deep love
for the Jewish religion through my journey with the Tree
of Life and the teachings of Kabbalah. I love the unique
metaphors for awakening expressed through the Jewish
tradition. They speak to my soul. I love that Kabbalah
uses duality to experience nonduality. The Tree of Life,
the ten sefirot, and the twenty-two paths between them
provide an extremely useful map to explore our human/
Divine life from exactly where we are, with the understanding that our human experience is never separate
from the whole.

In 2011, I decided to study for my bat mitzvah, forty-two years after my thirteenth birthday—the traditional age for this ceremony. I did this as a deep bow of gratitude to the Jewish adepts in my lineage.

Under the guidance of my local rabbi, Rabbi Arthur Gross-Schaeffer, I met weekly with four other women, who became dear friends, to learn the prayers and rituals of the Jewish religion. This gave me a new appreciation for the religion, but even with that, I have become only slightly more observant.

My spiritual life is anchored by my daily meditation practice, not in outer rituals. I returned to my religion as a monist, not a monotheist: my "God" is the One without second, the conceptless, nameless, both transcendent and immanent God. My God is also the intimate one, *Yechidah*, addressable by many names, closer than close, always within me.

Nevertheless, Judaism is very much about community, and with my "B'nai Mitzvah sisters," I found a container of love and support that kept me sane during the most stressful period of my life as those closest to me died.

Finally, on a glorious day in October 2013, I stood in front of family and friends and chanted my assigned portion from the Torah in Hebrew. I formally chose to stand with the Jewish people and receive the tradition of my ancestors.

These words inscribed on the ark that holds the Torah now had meaning for me: *She is a Tree of Life for those who hold fast to her* (Proverbs 3:18).

Yet my return would not have been possible without the advanced knowledge and specific spiritual practices imparted to me by Swamiji, Shivaji, and their lineage of Kundalini Science and Vedic teachings. Through these teachings, I welcomed and experienced the Divine feminine as the holy presence within. I experienced Kundalini Shakti/Shekinah as the initiator of true spiritual progress.

In today's world, where of out-of-control environmental abuse threatens to destroy our planet, where people act out their inner pain on the collective, and where violence is the preferred method of conflict resolution, the spiritual evolution of each person is what is needed for humanity to survive. Without it we remain in our egos, unable to source our direct connection to the Divine. When we truly know that there is no separation, that there is only One reality, only then will we be able to usher in the New Age.

In my last interview with Swamiji, he presented an article he had saved for me, describing the work of Rabbi Shefa Gold, who teaches Hebrew chant as a spiritual practice.

"You should study with her," he suggested.

I replied, "But, Swamiji, I can't sing!"

"No? Can't you learn?" he asked.

"Swamiji, people usually ask me not to sing. I don't think I could ever do it," I replied, and I let the idea go.

Then, this past Yom Kippur, I attended a chanting service that Rabbi Shefa Gold led in Los Angeles. For the first time in a Jewish service, I plunged as deeply into profound stillness as I do in my solitary meditation practice. I recalled Swamiji's recommendation and decided to sign up for her two-year training course, the Magic of Hebrew Chant.

The class was being held in a Catholic retreat center in Santa Fe, New Mexico. On the first morning, our group gathered outdoors, ironically under the horizontal and vertical arms of the cross, to chant the Hebrew prayer of gratitude, *Modah ani,* usually said upon awakening. The deeper meaning of the chant was not lost on me in that moment: I thanked God for the awakening of my soul.

Rabbi Shefa's translation of the Hebrew chant is:

I gratefully acknowledge your face.
Spirit lives and endures.
You return my soul to me with compassion.
How great is your faith in me!

Wrapped in my tallit, rocking and swaying to the chant, I experienced the same heartfelt devotion that I formerly felt while doing yogic chants. Tears streamed down my face as I opened to receive the grace flowing from the Hebrew words. A raven in the tree above cawed loudly, joining us in welcoming the day.

My deepest wish for you is that my spiritual experiences inspire you to make your own journey of return, to forge your own spiritual path, and that no matter what path you choose, you find that eventually all paths lead home.

Acknowledgments

I would like to acknowledge the following people, who were instrumental in the writing and completion of this book.

I express my deep gratitude to:

Instructor Shelly Lowenthal and the students in his memoir class, Adult Ed, Santa Barbara City College. You gave me the courage to start writing.

The members of my Mastermind group: Patricia Rachel Schwartz, MA, PCC; Madeleine Boskowitz, PhD; and Doreen Lerner, PhD. Without you, I would never have had the discipline to finish this book.

Marci Shimoff, for being my friend and traveler on this path and for writing the foreword.

Bri. Joan Shivarpita Harrigan, PhD (Shivaji), for your spiritual guidance, your compassion, and for the time you spent reviewing the chapters in the first draft of this book.

Nancy Marriott, for your encouragement and excellent editing of the first draft of the manuscript.

My family and friends, you know who you are; you have enriched my life with your company and have been my circle of love and support.

Barbara Brennan, David LaChapelle, Jason Shulman, Rabbi Sandy Roth, Rabbi Arthur Gross-Schaefer, and Rabbi Shefa Gold, for being my teachers.

Molly Green, for help with the illustrations.

My parents, Abe and Sandra Antman, thank you for your lifelong encouragement to pursue my dreams and for your constant support, even though my life turned out quite differently from what you may have imagined for me.

Allison McDaniel and the team at Turning Stone Press, thank you for improving my manuscript and helping me bring it to a higher standard of excellence.

Lastly, I express my eternal gratitude to the lineage of masters preserving the sacred spiritual science of Kundalini Vidya and to Swami Chandrasekharanand Saraswati and Joan Shivarpita Harrigan for bringing these teachings to the West.

Bibliography

Books

Alexander, Ram, *Death Must Die: A Western Woman's Life-Long Spiritual Quest in India with Shree Anandamayee Ma*, New Delhi, India: Indica Books, 2000, 2002, 2006.

Brennan, Barbara Ann, *Hands of Light*, New York City: Bantam Books, 1988.

Caplan, Mariana, *Eyes Wide Open, Cultivating Discernment on the Spiritual Path*, Boulder, Colorado: Sounds True, 2009.

Feldman, Daniel Hale, *Qabalah: The Mystical Heritage of the Children of Abraham*, California: Work of the Chariot, 2001.

Gitkatilla, Rabbi Joseph, *Gates of Light*, Lanham, Maryland: Alta Mira Press, 1994.

Gold, Rabbi Shefa, *The Magic of Hebrew Chant: Healing the Spirit, Transforming the Mind, Deepening Love*, Woodstock, Vermont: Jewish Lights Publishing, 2013.

Haich, Elisabeth, *Initiation*, Santa Fe, New Mexico: Aurora Press, 1974.

Harrigan, Joan Shivarpita, *Kundalini Vidya: The Science of Spiritual Transformation*, 6th ed., Knoxville, Tennessee: Patanjali Kundalini Yoga Care, 2005.

―――, *Stories of Spiritual Transformation: The Fulfillment of the Kundalini Process, Modern Seekers, Ancient Teachings*, Knoxville, Tennessee: Shakti Press, 2017.

Kaplan, Rabbi Aryeh, *Inner Space*, Brooklyn, New York: Moznaim Publishing Co., 1990.

————, *Sefer Yetzirah: Book of Creation, in Theory and Practice*, York Beach, Maine: Samuel Weiser, 1993.

Lannoy, Richard, *Anandamayi: Her Life and Wisdom*, Shaftesbury, England: Element Books Ltd., 1996.

Lipski, Alexander, *The Essential Sri Anandamayi Ma: Life and Teachings of a 20th Century Saint*, New Delhi, India: Motilal Banarsidass Publishers, 2007.

Parmahansa Yogananda, *Autobiography of a Yogi*, Los Angeles, California: Self-Realization Fellowship, 1946, 1974, 1981, 1990.

Shulman, Jason, *Kabbalistic Healing: A Path to an Awakened Soul*, Rochester, Vermont: Inner Traditions, 2004.

Websites

Dani Antman
www.daniantman.com
www.wiredforgod.com

Barbara Brennan School of Healing®
www.barbarabrennan.com

Patanjali Kundalini Yoga Care
www.kundalinicare.com

PKYC (India)
www.kundalini-science.ch

A Society of Souls®: (Now called: **The School for Non-Dual Healing and Awakening™**)
www.societyofsouls.com

Work of the Chariot
www.workofthechariot.com

Rabbi Shefa Gold
www.rabbishefagold.com

About the Author

As an internationally known energy healer and inter-faith minister in Santa Barbara, California, Dani Ant-man has been at the forefront of energy medicine and healing since 1992, when she graduated from the Bar-bara Brennan School of Healing. Dani was a senior teacher at The School for Nondual Healing and Awak-ening for over nine years, and has led workshops at the Esalen Institute, La Casa de Maria, and The Lionheart Institute for Transpersonal Energy Healing. She is dedi-cated to helping others progress on their spiritual path.

For more, visit www.wiredforgod.com.